NOTHING BUT. . .
CHRISTINE KEELER

NOTHING BUT. . .
CHRISTINE KEELER

Christine Keeler with Sandy Fawkes

NEW ENGLISH LIBRARY

A New English Library Original Publication, 1983

First NEL Paperback Edition March 1983

NEL Books are published by
New English Library,
Mill Road, Dunton Green,
Sevenoaks, Kent.
Editorial office: 47 Bedford Square, London WC1B 3DP

Typeset by Robcroft Ltd, London WC1
Made and printed in Great Britain by
Cox & Wyman Ltd, Reading

0 450 05564 7

PREFACE

You have opened this book because of the name on the cover. Christine Keeler. The words *scandal*, *tart*, *prostitute*, *Profumo*, any one of them could spring to mind. A lot has been written about the Christine Keeler case, a lot of it wrong. Not necessarily lies, but not the truth either. The time has come to tell the truth about the events behind the scenes in 1963 that led to the downfall of the Conservative government after twelve years in power. Some of the details are shocking, some are sad, some are funny, some are sordid. It is twenty years later and I am a grown woman, mature enough to let it all hang out.

The truth is that I liked sex, easy money and the high life. I was young and wild. I was naive, certainly. Innocent, no. Wicked? Find out for yourself.

CHAPTER ONE

SWEET SIXTEEN and never been kissed. Well, not exactly. But sweet sixteen I was, in London on my own; with a job as a dancer at Murrays Cabaret Club, a lost virginity, a desperately hideous abortion and several boyfriends behind me. And earning eight pounds ten shillings a week. That was a lot of money in 1958.

I had got the job through one of those chance encounters that were slowly, fatefully, to turn the name Christine Keeler into worldwide headline news and, so they say, to the downfall of the Conservative government.

I was living in a seedy boarding house and working as a waitress in a Greek restaurant in Baker Street when the most beautiful woman I had ever seen arrived. She was everything I wanted to be, glamorously dressed and made up, graceful and confident, laughing and conversing easily with both her companion and the waiters. She was a world apart; of stardom, magazine covers, of unchipped nail varnish and unladdered stockings. Grooming was still important in those days. I was astounded and flattered when she spoke to me as I cleared her table.

'Why don't you come along and meet Mr Murray, my boss, at the Cabaret Club?' she suggested. 'He's always looking for new talent and you have just the kind of looks he likes.'

'Me. What for?'

'As a dancer. The money is good, you meet interesting

people and you can have a lot of fun,' she added knowingly. 'I'll arrange for you to meet him. Why not give it a try?'

Why not indeed? I knew I was pretty, with my high cheekbones and large eyes. I had modelled for a clothes shop for a while (until I had broken a full length mirror and stepped on the boss's mother's toes), I had been photographed for *Titbits* and had been good at ballet until mum ran out of money for the lessons. So, a jumble of nerves, I went along for the interview.

The reality of a nightclub in daytime is a bit like waking up in bed with somebody you met at a party the night before. There is a sort of shabbiness about both situations and at that age I was inexperienced enough to be pathetically disappointed. Where were the glittering costumes? (Upstairs being patched by the wardrobe ladies). And what about the soft lights, the sweet music and the romance?

I paraded in a borrowed leotard before Mr Murray, who looked like a city gent in a double-breasted striped suit, bespectacled and balding. As I tried out a few steps, copying Maureen my friend from the Greek restaurant, I wanted to run like hell before I was turned down.

'Right, that's it, enough,' shouted Mr Murray, 'You're hired.'

I couldn't believe it, it was fantastic, fabulous and impossible. I was on my way to stardom. I started rehearsals; I wasn't to be a dancer yet but a topless showgirl. A few days later I made my debut in silver shoes, a glittering G-string and an enormous head-dress of feathers and sequins, carrying a lantern. I loved it. I loved working there at first, it was fun to work with so many girls, we gossiped and giggled, and at last I felt as if I belonged somewhere. And I learned a lot listening to all the talk from the girls who had been around a lot longer than me.

Nightclubs were expected to provide glamour, literally

for 'the tired businessman' in those days. Between shows we were invited to sit and talk with the customers, though now wearing our pretty flouncy evening dresses. There were two shows a night and it is ironic now to think that the signature tune that signified it was time for us to return to work was 'That's Why the Lady is a Tramp'.

Now a lot of rot has been written about Mr Murray and his Cabaret Club. How we were all such sedate young ladies obeying the club rules and being threatened with instant dismissal if we ever made a date outside the premises. Absolute rubbish, as I soon discovered. Any rules made to prevent the suggestion of hanky panky going on at the club were made to protect the reputation of the paying customers, not ours. Discretion is the polite word for hypocrisy and most of us made after-hours arrangements to meet the gentlemen we had been playing hostess to. And we got paid for our services. Very discreetly of course, a bundle of fivers 'for the taxi home, my dear' or 'to buy yourself a little present'. The money went on clothes, hairdos, make-up, taxis and just having fun. Of course Percy Murray knew what we were up to, it was he who arranged which girl would sit at which table, though there was never any pressure to oblige. And he knew what we were charging. I should know. He used to bed me once or twice a week and there was always an extra fifteen quid in my hand afterwards and I wasn't the only one. But he would never have dreamed of asking for a cut, he was a gentleman.

There was also the extra fiver to be earned just chatting to the customers. Luckily my stepfather had taught me to speak well and a lot of the men (who seemed impossibly old in my eyes) only wanted to talk about their problems. Money was easy all round – this was the time when Harold Macmillan had made his famous statement, 'You've never had it so good' – and we were determined to prove him

3

right. So I drifted into accepting money for sex and the girls at the club used to laugh at the ones who pretended they didn't. I didn't feel in the least bit guilty about it.

At the club I met a very nice young man, an ex-public schoolboy and rising young executive, truly tall, dark and handsome – and fun. His name was Michael Lambton and he was very enamoured of me and spent lavishly at the club. As he became more involved he begged me to leave my job and live with him. It was tempting because London, and particularly Chelsea where he lived, was beginning to come to life. Smart little restaurants where Michael and his friends congregated for an evening of fun were springing up and in comparison to that life spending my evenings listening to old men talking about themselves was becoming boring. I began to play hookey with Michael and, since we were always fined for not turning up, my pay packet began to dwindle. Michael, of course, knew nothing of the other side of my life and I soon realised that I needed Murrays more than I needed him. I wasn't in love, I didn't dislike sex, and I liked the money it brought in.

There was a rich Arab, Ahmed Kanu, who was one of my regulars from the club. Some of his young rich Arab friends threw marvellous parties after the club closed at 3 a.m. and the girls and myself would go there to wind down and have a laugh. They weren't orgies though some of us would stay the night.

One evening Mr Murray came backstage to tell me that Ahmed was in with some friends and would like me to join them. That was the way of the club, the girls never wandered around or sat at the bar waiting for a pick-up. The invitations had to come from the customers and the decisions were made by Mr Murray. If a customer looked like he might be drunk enough to be a nuisance, for instance, the young ladies were not available.

And that was how I came to meet Stephen Ward. He was

there with a starlet and I was to make up the foursome. Stephen was full of praise for the floorshow and admiration for me. He asked me to dance and, holding me tight, asked 'What are you doing later?'

I was used to that old routine by now and applied the house rules. Drawing back ever so politely I replied, 'I am going home.'

'I'll take you home if you like,' he suggested casually.

'Oh no, that's impossible, I really must go home alone.' I was meeting a very nice young Greek later and I wasn't going to let some old man – Stephen was at least forty – spoil my evening.

'Do men sometimes take you home?' Stephen was smiling at me hopefully. 'I must have your phone number,' he persisted.

This was always a tricky moment and we often gave fictional numbers just to keep them happy. I was hesitant. Why on earth should I bother? I thought. I shall never see you outside this place.

'Ah, Christine, you are a very sweet person, you know,' he murmured as he ushered me back to the table. 'I think you and I are going to be friends for a very long time.' It was said to me so often I could have no premonition that he was speaking the truth and that the Fates were on the move again. As it was, the words went in one ear and out the other.

Back at the table Stephen continued to focus all his attention on me, ignoring his date and infuriating Ahmed who was, like many men from the Middle East, very possessive. The tension at the table soon became obvious and Stephen recognised that he and his guest had better leave, but he maintained his good-natured cool.

'I must have your phone number before I leave, I really would like to ring you,' he continued to insist, and I could see he was in earnest despite his cheerful manner. I realised that the sooner I gave it to him the quicker he would go. I mumbled my number hoping he wouldn't catch it, but he was smart all right, he had notebook and pen at the ready. He wrote it down and with a courteous nod to Ahmed, wished him a pleasant evening and left with his starlet.

And although I did not know it, the pattern of our relationship was set. Stephen could charm anyone into doing exactly what he wanted them to do.

I thought no more of it. Many men under the influence of a good dinner and champagne convince themselves that they have either met their hearts' delight or made a conquest until they wake up to the sober light of day. The scribbled number probably ends up in their waste paper basket the following morning. So I was surprised when Stephen rang, not just once but three times the next day. I refused his invitations to join him for a coffee but over our chats on the phone I learned that he was an osteopath and had a practice in Wimpole Street. He would ring me while he was waiting for a client to turn up and I told him it was too darn early for me to put my face on and go out to meet anyone, I was working from nine in the evening till three in the morning. The last excuse I made was to tell him that I was off to see my mum for the weekend which was true. Stephen wanted to know where I lived and I told him that it was a village called Wraysbury. He knew the area well, even the street next to the lane I lived in, so he wished me a happy weekend and said he would ring next week.

I loved my mum and still do, but I had left Wraysbury because I couldn't get on with my stepfather, a fairly typical situation that drives young girls to London to seek their fortune. We lived in a couple of converted railway carriages, not because it was the smart thing to do but because we were too poor to afford a bungalow. I was by nature a rebellious tomboy which didn't help a lot. Funny really to think that the girl who became the wicked sex

6

symbol of the Sixties was the best discus and javelin thrower at the school and got up at six o'clock each morning to do a paper round on a home-made bike that had no brakes. No wonder I liked the easy money.

Dad was strict to the point of bullying. 'She'll end up no good,' he used to say to mum – and I proved him right by getting pregnant at the age of fifteen. I couldn't tell them and did all the usual dangerous things that scared young girls do: gin and hot baths, castor oil and finally the horrible self probing with the knitting needle. And alone in my bunk in the caravan I finally aborted at six months. Hell, agonising hell was where I was at, the pain tearing and surging at me. 'Mum, mum, mum,' I cried out for the first time because I had seen it. There was the horrible reality. A slimy mauve and red head, there, not there and there again. Mum heard my call and cycled away for the doctor. My first child was born, a pathetic, withered, half-living thing. They took him to the hospital where he died six days later and after that there was no sleep, no peace, nothing but pain and shame. I couldn't stay home after that.

So you can imagine how I felt when I saw Stephen walking up the path to our little home on the Saturday morning. By now I was reconciled to my stepfather and in later years was to be deeply grateful for his support, but right then I was horrified to be discovered in my humble home. After all I was now a glamorous figure, I earned good money, I was a dancer in the West End meeting the new television stars, famous showbiz names. My two lives could not possibly mix.

'Hello Christine,' said Stephen, taking everything in at once. 'I was just passing and thought I'd drop in. I've got a little cottage not far from here and thought you might like a drive.'

I could hardly close the door in his face so I invited him in for a cup of tea. Mum was delighted because I had never introduced any of my new friends before. 'What a charming little place you have here,' he said with that vital enthusiasm Stephen had for everything around him. He meant it too and instantly made my parents feel at ease. He strode to the window. 'And what a lovely view,' he said.

'Yes, everyone thinks the view is good,' said dad. He was being affable while mum fussed around putting the kettle on and fishing the cups out of the sink. 'And we've got a river running along the back.'

'How absolutely marvellous. My cottage at Cliveden is on the river too. I was hoping to take Christine to see it this afternoon.'

Dad and Stephen went down the garden to admire the river while I tried to pull myself together. Seeing him so instantly at home with my parents and hearing his charming voice again had left me confused. I think mum was already match-making.

'What a lovely man he is, Chris, where did you meet him?'

'He came to the club the other night and he's been ringing me ever since, I can't seem to get rid of him.'

'Well I think he is very nice, so friendly.'

'He wants to take me for a drive to see his cottage,' I said doubtfully. I thought I could guess what he was after and thought that mum might disapprove. Also I didn't fancy him.

'Why ever don't you?' Mum was surprised that I could refuse an invitation from such a nice gentleman. At that moment Stephen returned, tripping on the step and laughing at his own clumsiness. Over tea Stephen told them how wonderful he thought I was at the club and repeated his invitation to visit Cliveden but this time addressing himself to mum as if asking permission. Mum was all on his side and any reluctance I felt was soon brushed away.

'I think you are a very lucky girl to have such a nice man

taking an interest in you, Chris, I only wish I'd had the same when I was your age.'

Stephen was pleased, he could tell he had impressed my parents, so he went on.

'London is a shocking place, especially for a girl with Christine's looks, and there are a lot of very undesirable types about who would be only too pleased to exploit her. In London you need to know the right people to help you go in the right direction.'

Mum was even more impressed by now. I had acquired a protector, someone who was going to introduce me to wealthy and important people. And how right she was, alas. It was a gorgeous day and as we drove through the villages and byways I found myself feeling relaxed and happy in Stephen's company.

He told me he rented the cottage from Lord Astor, who was both a friend and a patient, and that he'd had the cottage for about eight years. As we drove through the magnificent grounds he explained that they were run by the National Trust because even the nobility could no longer afford the upkeep.

'Many very famous people visit here and always have done,' he said. 'It is one of the few country seats still in power. Bill entertains royalty, diplomats and politicians, he probably wields a lot of power just like in the olden days. I should think a lot of behind-the-scenes governmental deals go on up at the house but he is a very, very friendly man.'

I was too busy admiring the view to take much notice. I wasn't interested in either power or politics and couldn't conceive the kind of money that went with property like this. I was entering a dream world and was expecting to see a picture-book cottage with roses round the door any minute. Instead of which we drew up in front of a house that was a mansion in my eyes. It was tall and gabled and the river ran right by it.

9

'But it's huge,' I said to Stephen.

'Not really,' said Stephen nonchalantly. 'But come in and have a look round.'

It was a strange house: the first room we entered was large, light, beautiful and totally empty. 'I must furnish it sometime,' he said casually, but he never did. The kitchen was the hub of the house. It astonished me to see a place so well equipped and so stacked with food, a complete contrast to my own background of cramped quarters and small gas stoves. I asked him if he lived here all the time.

'No, no, just weekends, but I hardly eat during the week and I usually invite a group of people down so I like to be able to cook for them; it's fun.'

I was still a bit bewildered while he made the coffee and then he said he wanted to draw me. I was flattered and sat desperately still, hardly daring to breathe, and all the while he told me about himself. How he had travelled to America as a cook on a boat, then scraped a living together to learn osteopathy. It was funny really, because even while he was talking about his early poverty, perhaps to make me feel more comfortable about my own humble origins, he still could not help name-dropping. He told me that he had painted most of the members of the Royal Family, that people like Prince Philip and Winston Churchill had visited him. It was all very exciting.

And he didn't make a pass at me. As the daylight faded he popped me into his car and drove me safely home. I was dying to tell mum all about it, bubbling with enthusiasm.

'You're a very lucky girl,' she told me solemnly. 'You keep hold of him.'

Well, that wasn't difficult because he was on the phone all the time and finally I agreed to get out of bed and meet him at a coffee bar in Marylebone High Street before I went to work. He was still chatting on about his famous friends and said he would like to introduce me to some of them but

10

that it would be impossible while I was still working at the club, as I had no free evenings. I protested that I loved my work and he suggested that I could earn more money and have more freedom if I became a model. He would do all he could to help. I told him that I had already given that a try and the comic disasters that had accompanied my first job; treading on the boss's mum's foot and breaking the mirror made him fall about laughing.

'And,' I said severely, 'the manager kept trying to grope me in dark corners.'

'Dirty old devil, men really are bastards.'

I looked at Stephen and wondered if he was a dirty old bastard and decided that he wasn't.

'Are you married, Stephen?'

'Good God, no,' he laughed and quickly changed the subject. 'Why did you leave home, Christine?'

'I didn't get on with my stepfather.' It was my turn to change the subject.

That night at the club I told Michael all about Stephen, partly to tease him into recognising that I had other beaux, partly to check Stephen out. I knew I was gullible and half suspected that Stephen might be taking advantage of my lack of knowledge of London life. Michael had never heard of Stephen Ward and dismissed him quickly but he rose to the bait.

'Is he a new boyfriend?'

'Don't be silly, he's far too old. But I think he is lonely.' And I told him about the cottage on the grand estate with its empty room and over-stocked kitchen waiting for guests to arrive. Once Michael was assured that I was not interested in Stephen as a boyfriend he was indifferent, but then he was always rude about people he didn't know. 'Sounds like a crank to me,' was all he said.

Stephen's charm was insidious; he could sense a

weakness and he knew how to play on it. He rang the next day to invite me for a coffee at that same cafe. Weakly I tried to get out of it, mumbling about a boyfriend and having to go to work.

'Give it a miss,' said Stephen cheerfully down the phone. 'It's a lovely day and a beautiful girl like you deserves some life of her own.'

He was right, of course. Spending my evenings talking to old men about their dividends could not compare with Stephen's wickedly witty gossip about people in high places. And for some reason Stephen treated me like a human being, an equal, instead of something to be groped and leered at. I met him and we sat outside chatting happily in the sun.

'Why don't you come and live with me?' It was a question out of the blue and an even more unlikely proposition than Michael's. 'I've only got a small place but you're out from nine in the evening and I'm out all day so we wouldn't get in each other's way.'

'But I already have a place,' I replied. How could he ask? He was obviously far too old for me and hadn't even made any sexual overtures. It was absurd.

'Never mind, come and see my place anyway.' Again it was as casual yet persuasive as the invitation to visit his cottage. He could make anything sound like an adventure, however small, and also that it was silly, childish, to refuse. So once again I clambered into his car and off we drove to Orme Court in South Kensington. If I was expecting a repeat experience of Cliveden I was in for a surprise. His flat was a tiny bed-sitting room with two single beds pushed close together, but he had an adjoining luxurious bathroom with one of those long, deep, old-fashioned baths. I just wanted to climb in and wallow. There was a bathroom in the railway carriage but no running hot water and the one at the boarding house was shared by all the tenants and always filthy, like the rest of the place really, a morbid, miserable hole. While Stephen put the kettle on for the inevitable cup of coffee – he drank it all day and smoked incessantly – I admired his neat and tidy home. I reached automatically for the cups and everything seemed so natural, we were a team.

'How many sugars?' I asked.

'Two, little baby, always two. I wish you would come and live here, I honestly feel as if I have known you for years already.'

He was so easy to talk to. Unlike most people he listened and you never had to repeat a name twice. As I washed up the cups and put them back in their place I felt at home, but when he reiterated his wish that I would move in with him I replied cautiously, 'I'll have to think about it. I'm not very sexy you know.'

'I don't want to make love to you, silly, I just like your company.'

In retrospect, of course, it was an odd proposition; an 'old' man living with a young girl with no sexual involvement. A more unlikely state of affairs is difficult to imagine. And yet it worked. I had thought for a day about his suggestion and the more I thought the more beguiling the idea became. He was so alive and enthusiastic about life, so amusing and spontaneous. His conversation rippled with titles yet he could be tremendously kind if someone was floundering at a party; he would rescue them with a quick joke and cover any possible embarrassment. He was carefree and flippant and wanted the world around him to have the same attitude.

He was also insatiably curious about other people's lives. Every night when I got home he would be sitting up reading, usually thrillers or Dennis Wheatley, waiting to hear about my evening. Who had been in with whom, what had been said, who had made a pass at me and who did I fancy? So I passed on the club gossip. In those days a great deal of it was about abortions: the Pill was only available to respectably married ladies and even they had to have the permission of their husbands, so one or other of us were invariably In Trouble. There was an obliging man in Harley Street and the customers would always prefer to pay up rather than be found out. It all seemed like a laugh at the time, particularly as Stephen usually knew the details of their respectable backgrounds.

One night I came home to find Stephen in a high old state of excitement, I had hardly got through the door before he was pulling me in with a conspiratorial whisper.

'Little baby, you should have heard the goings-on next door tonight. What a fight! It's a prostitute and her ponce, he was hitting her and she was screaming, calling him every name under the sun.' His face was alive with excitement. I was curious to know what he had done about it but at that moment the hollering started again. 'Quick, pass me that glass,' said Stephen. I did and he turned it, the open end up against the wall, his ear pressed close.

'You can hear every word this way,' he whispered. 'Ah, she's demanding her money now, telling him what a cunt he is, ooh, he's walloped her again, and she's calling him a lying bastard and a thieving pimp.' He was all attention, his ear glued to the glass. 'Ooh, he's groaning now, he's in agony, I think she must have kicked him in the balls. Must have hurt because he's leaving. He's threatening her. "I'll be back later," he said. There, there's the door, quick, little baby, run to the window and see if you can see him go.'

Stephen put the glass down, holding his stomach and his mouth with laughter, doubled up. I started to laugh too – there was always something so infectious about Stephen that you couldn't actually worry about other people's problems. They were all just part of the entertainment. I suppose it was round about then that I came to realise that

Stephen got most of his sexual thrills second-hand.

Once or twice at the beginning of our relationship Stephen had tried to find out whether I would be interested in him sexually but he always left a way out for me to refuse. Our relationship became one of brother and sister, perhaps emotionally incestuous, but it didn't appear to me in any way sinister. We were happy together. It was through Stephen that I heard about the orgies that were the rage in upper-crust London round about 1960, long before wife-swapping became a popular sport in the suburbs. He told me that he couldn't get a hard-on at these occasions but didn't object to stripping off in order to watch. His accounts were riotous.

One evening Stephen insisted I accompany him to dinner with some friends who lived in Maida Vale. I was still working at Murrays, but I was becoming very influenced by Stephen and, if I was enjoying myself, would risk the ten shilling fine that resulted from being late. So off we went to dinner with these friends whom he had so vividly described.

'Well, my little baby, they believe that having sex with other people around keeps their marriage alive. Bertie and Mary came to the cottage one weekend and there was Bertie having it off with a girl and Mary was having it off with another man and all Bertie was interested in was whether his wife was enjoying herself with the other fellow. It makes you think, little baby, perhaps that's what it's all about.'

It didn't make me think too much. I was still at the stage of falling passionately in love, not for long admittedly, but if I was wild for someone they had to be mine alone.

One of the nice things about Stephen was that he liked me to look myself. In those days of piled-up beehive hairstyles I wore my dark hair long and loose, and with my waspie pulled in tight to emphasise my splendid waist, and my eyes made up, I had made myself look very glamorous for this great occasion. When we arrived at the door we were laughing with excitement and the anticipation of not knowing what was going to happen.

There were six of us altogether. The other guests were introduced as Carol and John. It was a beautiful house filled with flowers and big mirrors, the mantelpiece was stacked with gold embossed invitations to grand parties and embassy balls and everyone was dressed up looking as if they were ready to be photographed for the *Tatler*. We had cocktails and then went into dinner and there, right in the centre of the gleaming dining room table, was an enormous plastic penis. We arranged ourselves politely in our places and for a moment I wondered if perhaps they had made a mistake. But not for long. Stephen was the first to mention it.

'Very handsome,' he was laughing. 'Where did you get it?'

'Germany,' replied our host.

'And what do you think of that, little baby?' said Stephen, deliberately drawing attention to me.

I smiled back brightly, non-committally – after all, it may have looked odd in amongst the Georgian silver and the fine china but I had seen one before.

'Mary and I came across them in Germany through a friend,' continued Bertie. 'They come in all shapes and sizes, they have even got them with hairs on.'

'And one with a dragon's spine at the end,' interrupted Mary excitedly.

'What if you'd got caught coming through the customs, there'd have been a hell of a rumpus. Remember poor old Eugene Goossens at Sydney airport. What would have been said?'

'Simple, old boy, got it all worked out. I'd have told 'em mine got shot off in the war and this is for my wife's convenience. It is too, isn't it, darling? She uses them on

16

her girlfriends,' he explained to the rest of the guests.

'Just look at the size of it, Christine,' said Stephen, mischief-making again. I wasn't quite sure what to do. I wasn't bold enough to say anything, but any other reaction would have been greeted with laughter, so once again I smiled politely. One thing about being out with Stephen, you didn't have to talk much, he did it all; and all the while I supposed this was how everybody who lived in grand houses behaved.

'Christine is a very sweet little girl,' Stephen was saying, covering up for my lack of conversation. 'She works at Murrays Club.'

'And I have to be there at nine-thirty.'

'In that case, my dear, we shall finish dinner a little earlier than usual.' Mary managed to look both gracious and gleeful. I didn't know quite what to make of it and I knew even less ten minutes later when she left the room and returned wearing nothing but a grass skirt with about ten straws hanging from it. What do you do? Laugh? Look the other way? Or do what everyone else was doing – taking their clothes off while the host and Stephen unfolded the sofa to make an enormous bed. Even Stephen was taking his trousers off but all those old men stripping didn't turn me on one bit.

'Off with your clothes, Christine,' commanded Stephen. So I did, except for my bra, though I don't think they were interested in tits anyway.

Bertie was already on top of Carol, the girl John had brought with him, and Stephen was just standing there laughing as Bertie then dragged me down as well, grabbing at my breasts. I remember thinking, fancy having it off with one person and playing with someone else's tits at the same time, then, well it's different, not what I'd call sexy but different, especially as it was all in daylight. Bertie was on to me next but I didn't want him to put his cock inside me so

17

he went down on me which I enjoyed so much I wanted him to finish me off inside, which he did very thoroughly. I came. Then I had had enough. Stephen had been standing there watching all the time, loving it, and so had I while it was going on but afterwards I felt embarrassed.

Then our gracious hostess, Mary, went down on me and once again, I admit, I was enjoying it, though I did notice that she hadn't brought the cock from the dining table. By this time Stephen had joined in too, going down on the hostess; we were just a mass of heaving bodies. Mary reached out for a whip and gave it to Stephen who stood over us, Mary still making me come like mad. 'You naughty little baby,' he said, and he brought the whip down hard on my stomach.

That I couldn't take. It bloody hurt. And furthermore the marks would show when I stripped off for my act. I was going, and I grabbed my clothes as quickly as I could. Stephen was very apologetic but the others were too busy to notice.

'Christine has to go now,' he announced.

They looked up briefly and called goodbye. 'See you again soon, we hope,' and then they were all back at it again. Stephen saw me to the door and stood there quite naked for all the world to see. I told him I didn't really like orgies.

'You're too self-conscious, little baby, don't think so much about it, bodies are only bodies, we've all got them, might as well enjoy them. You aren't annoyed are you? You do still want to live with me?'

Of course I did, I couldn't imagine living with anyone else.

'Look, little baby, I think I can afford to get us a larger place, perhaps a house even, would you like that?'

'But I love our little home.'

'Yes, but if we had a house we could entertain.' My face

must have shown my thoughts because he laughed. 'No, no, not orgies, I promise you. Bridge parties and just friends dropping in . . . we could even get married.' It was casually said and I knew there would be no pressure till I felt certain. 'We would have the ideal marriage, we could both do just as we pleased, no jealousies, no questions, yet have each other. Tell you what we'll do, we'll start looking for a house tomorrow and we'll find one big enough for you to have your own room. I know just the person to go to, a man I met recently, he's got a lot of property, his name is Peter Rachman.'

In the taxi back to Murrays that night I had to laugh. There was I, a country lass from Buckinghamshire, and I had been to an orgy in a posh house where the silver on the table would have kept my parents for the rest of their lives. I had had sex with a lady of quality and had been proposed to by a naked man. I was really beginning to learn about High Society.

CHAPTER TWO

PETER RACHMAN was a strange person. Like Stephen he laughed a lot but his eyes never for a moment lost their cold, glittering hardness.

When Stephen telephoned Rachman about a house Peter suggested we met up for a drink at his flat in Bryanston Mews West, close to Park Lane. As we set off, Stephen told me that Peter Rachman was a Polish exile who owned vast amounts of property in London and had interests in several clubs and restaurants. At that time I think even Stephen, who knew most things about everyone, had no idea exactly how Peter had made his fortune – it was still very respectable to be a property dealer. And if he had he probably wouldn't have been shocked: he would have reasoned that at least Peter was providing the great influx of West Indians with roofs over their heads at a time when the middle-class masses were extremely anxious that such people should not move into their area lest it lowered the value of their own property.

But none of that was at all evident as Peter introduced us to his partner for the evening, Cherie, a poised and elegant girl whom I liked immediately. Over drinks Stephen described what we were looking for, a small flat not too far from his consulting rooms in Harley Street. Peter suggested that we discussed it over dinner. Stephen and I brightened up immediately. I suppose we were both a couple of scroungers really because we did like a free supper.

Stephen was far too mean to pay, although he was generosity itself in the country. We went to a club run by Toomy Yeardye and while the men talked Cherie and I escaped to the ladies for a chat.

She asked me if I would like to come round for tea the following afternoon, an invitation I gladly accepted as it would make a pleasant change from spending the day alone while Stephen was at work, and besides that she promised to teach me how to wear false eyelashes like herself. I thought they were the epitome of glamour. I didn't know till much later that the idea had come from Peter. The next day, as Cherie, who was a trained Lucie Clayton model, showed me how to apply my make-up professionally, we talked about our love-lives and our work. She was very curious about my life with Stephen and I was equally curious about hers with Peter. She explained that although the flat was Peter's she lived there in order to be able to see her lover, Raymond Nash, who was married and also connected with Peter through gambling clubs.

Peter arrived during the afternoon and we played chess, a game my stepfather had taught me well enough for Peter to be impressed with my ability. I was enjoying myself, there was classical music playing, a lot of laughter, and I felt a bit like Cinderella when I announced that I had to go to get ready for work. It was seven in the evening.

Peter was visibly shocked. 'What kind of work can you be going to at this time of night?'

I explained to him that I was a dancer at the Cabaret Club.

'But I thought you lived with Stephen, that's why you want a flat. I know Stephen has a reputation for meanness but surely he must keep you?'

It was a perfectly rational reaction. Girls only worked until they found a husband or at least a protector. They were not expected to go Dutch except perhaps among students, and certainly not in Peter's world. Rather lamely I tried to tell them about our home arrangement. Peter became even more bemused and the more I tried to describe our circumstances the more indignant he became.

'In that case you should be sharing with a girl, and with your looks you should be looking towards modelling, not wearing yourself out working those sort of hours at a club, it's ridiculous. Now, you move in with Cherie, she will help you find some work and I will lend you a few bob to get started, but you must leave the club.'

It was all very enticing. Cherie was enthusiastic, she was lonely as she did not see much of her handsome lover and it would be fun to live in luxurious surroundings with a girl of my own age. But what to say to Stephen? The answer was nothing, I was too much of a coward and a couple of days later I packed my things, left Orme Court, and moved into Bryanston Mews.

No indication of my obligations had been made at the tea party but when, on the day I arrived, Peter grabbed me and led me into the bedroom I just let him do it and from then on that was how it was every afternoon.

Sex to Peter Rachman was like cleaning his teeth and I was the toothpaste. It wasn't pleasant, it wasn't unpleasant; it was perfunctory, impersonal, and purely for his own pleasure. He never kissed and he never went down. He would arrive and without ceremony take me roughly by the arm and push me in front of him towards the bedroom. I never saw his face while we had sex as he always made me sit on top of him facing the other way. It did not concern him if the girl involved enjoyed herself or not; the feminist demand for orgasm that grew so vociferous in the Sixties would probably have puzzled him, for all the emotion had been bludgeoned out of him in his early years as he fought for survival in Russian concentration camps. For him there was no such thing as give and take in life – what was his was his and watch out anyone who didn't pay their dues or tried to take anything away from him.

And that included the likes of me. Beautiful girls were part of his chattels, and he liked to flaunt his financial power to the world. Consequently I was thoroughly spoiled with expensive clothes and plenty of money to spend on make-up and at the hairdressers, all so that when he swept into a restaurant with Cherie and myself on each arm everyone would envy him. For a while I loved being kept, and being part of the idle rich suited me fine, for Peter always carried a roll of two or three hundred pounds on him and liked to be seen spending it.

Wherever he went he was well known. This was partly due to the fact that he would only patronise a restaurant if he could inspect the kitchens. He was paranoiac about cleanliness, and the management, doubtless with an eye on his bankroll, tolerated the fact that he must always wash his own glass before he drank from it. It was a leftover of the horrors he had suffered as a youth when he had seen people actually eat German excrement.

He never introduced either Cherie or I to any of his friends or acquaintances; that was also part of his possessiveness, he could not imagine a man and a woman having a platonic relationship. Women were there to be cosseted, to be decorative and to be screwed. And that was the end of the matter.

I probably met some of the biggest villains in London of the time but since they all wore the same expensively tailored suits as the men I had met at Murrays I couldn't tell the difference. Peter would sometimes talk business on the phone at the flat but I never heard him doing anything like ordering the dogs in, though later the newspapers reported that he used vicious tactics to evict tenants. I knew he had a Polish friend with two Alsatians and once, when we were playing chess as we often did after sex, he told me that the man was a trained assassin in the Polish resistance who had killed a woman, a traitor, at the age of fourteen. Apparently the woman, sensing that he was a virgin, had offered him a screw in exchange for her life but he shot her just the same.

Peter hated all Germans, for obvious reasons, but he hated the blacks even more. I can only suppose it was because he had been treated like shit, like the lowest of the low, so when he got the chance to kick someone he felt was even lower than himself, he took it. Curious really, his hatred was genuine and deep, and yet during those early years of the immigrant influx he *was* the only person prepared to provide homes for them and those who could pay were very grateful

When Stephen discovered what I was up to he was furious with both Peter and myself. 'You will ruin your reputation being seen around with a man like that and the company he keeps,' he screamed at me. Peter brushed this aside and told me that Stephen was behaving like a silly, bitchy old woman, full of jealousy. I was enjoying the easy money but getting a little restless.

For one thing, Cherie was being made very unhappy by her handsome Raymond. She came from a wealthy family and was passionately in love with him, but he treated her like dirt. If he felt like seeing her he would just bang on the door at any hour of the night and I would have to get out of the double bed we shared and sleep on the sofa. One night he gave us the fright of our lives by breaking in through the bedroom window because we had not heard the doorbell. He was often violent too.

Peter never slept a night at the flat so spending evening after evening tied down keeping Cherie cheerful began to pall. Peter soon sensed this and hurriedly invented a new lure to keep me; my very own white sports car so that I could visit my parents each weekend. My stepfather had taught me to drive at a very early age (a bit like how he had taught me to swim: he'd shown me how it worked, shut me in the driving seat and threatened me with a walloping if I damaged his car, and trivialities like passing a driving test didn't cross my mind).

At first this was a very happy arrangement. I loved my new freedom and as soon as Peter left each day I would buzz round London visiting friends and seeing Stephen again. Needless to say I soon started taking advantage of this freedom by seeing an early boyfriend of mine, another Peter, younger and lustier, from my village. Equally needless to say, Rachman's possessiveness soon turned to brooding suspiciousness about what I was up to in his absence and he put his hoods on to me. I could be just out for some fresh air but a heavy car would cut across me and wave me down, I would be told in no uncertain manner to go home immediately and I did. Peter was a dangerous man to upset though he was never violent to me. He would punch the wall and call me 'Little Bastard', then laugh at himself. He didn't want to lose me and I knew it.

'If I ever find you fucking another man I'll chuck you out,' he would scream in his high pitched Polish voice, then take me round to Maurice Krevatz, his tailor, and order me a whole set of new clothes just to make sure I knew which side my bread was buttered.

The crunch came when I started to spend long weekends with my parents, having it off with my sweetheart which I enjoyed for two reasons. One was his lovely, young, ardent body, the other was that his parents had always disapproved of me and I was now rich, smart, and the best dressed girl in the village. I lied like the proverbial trooper each Monday when I returned to London, not even letting Cherie into my secret, I really thought I had got the world on a string, an old man to keep me in luxury and a young man to please me. But I was wrong, as I found out one

Saturday when Rachman got one of his 'boys' to drive him to Wraysbury unexpectedly. He found Peter and I larking about with a group of friends outside the pub.

'Give me the car keys,' he shouted in front of them all.

Humiliated and furious, I did so. There was no arguing with him.

'And if you come back,' he said, very pointedly, 'see that you behave yourself.'

I decided not to go back. The eternal gypsy in me rebelled. I had lived with him for six months, I had grown to like him even though I realised that he was a very unscrupulous man, but I was fed up with being owned.

I rang Stephen, of course, who was delighted to have me back. He had moved to a little house in Wimpole Mews (without the help of Mr Rachman) and there was a spare bedroom all waiting for me. And, despite his fury and disappointment, Peter allowed me to collect my clothes and gifts from Bryanston Mews.

So I launched myself back into my old London life. I persuaded Percy Murray to let me return to the Cabaret Club, though he punished me by relegating me to the back row for a while which made me very indignant. I met up with Michael Lambton again, the Arab boys were still giving wild parties in Belgravia and I was soon spending the weekends and days with Stephen at Cliveden.

I was refreshed and happy, as was Stephen who was as good as his word about using his home to entertain. There was nothing formal, people just knocked on the door when they felt like a chat and a cup of coffee. Stephen was still too mean to keep drink in the house. Many of the visitors were patients of Stephen, quite a lot of them were titled, they were all around Stephen's age but, as I rarely read newspapers, their names meant nothing to me. After the introductions I would soon wander off into my own room; doing my own thing was of more interest to me than listening to their conversation.

Occasionally Stephen would tell me that I had just met someone like Sir Oswald Mosley or Sir Godfrey Nicholson, and I am fairly sure that Anthony Blunt was a regular visitor, but mostly their names, and the power they held, were way above my head. Nobody ever stayed very long. Sometimes Stephen would get out his sketch pad while they were talking and I suppose some of his sitters may have been flattered into telling more than they should during these sessions. Certainly the tone was always serious, not sparkling gossip about sex.

But there was one guest who I always wished would stay longer, a tall, handsome, utterly charming Russian, Eugene Ivanov. Stephen told me that he was the Assistant Naval Attaché at the Russian Embassy and they had met at a bridge party. To me he was an exotic, glamorous figure, with impeccable manners; even so, he managed to convey to me that girls like myself did not fit into his scheme of thinking, that he was there only to collect Stephen to take him to the bridge club. To get away from this heady atmosphere I occasionally stayed with a girlfriend, Jenny, who was the lead dancer at Murrays. I had no time to pine, I was working at Murrays every night, on my best behaviour in order to get out of the back row and up to my old tricks again. Most of the girls took off from time to time so Percy always had a steady turnover of new girls, hopefully on their way to fame and fortune, and I soon noticed one of them in particular, mostly because she looked so common. Her name was Mandy Rice-Davies. Now there is nothing quite so superior as a newly confident nineteen-year-old faced with a beginner of sixteen. Cherie had passed on to me all she had learned at Lucy Clayton's about make-up so I considered Mandy's thick pancake foundation and bilious, bright green eye-shadow very vulgar. Very haughty I was. I didn't like her at first but she was popular with the Arabs and it always turned out that the two of us would be invited to their parties.

Mandy and I soon fell into the habit of staying at the Arabs' flat with two of the men we fancied. It was so much easier than going home. Mandy had a room in Swiss Cottage and I had mine with Stephen but it was more fun to spend the day and travel to work together. I took charge of Mandy, teaching her how to do her face and giving her a lot of the expensive clothes Peter had bought me; my great age and experience assured that I was the boss. Once again I had a girlfriend to giggle with. We complemented each other perfectly; Mandy was bold and I was shy, Mandy was mercenary, clever about money and I was a bit of a dreamer about it – like Mr Micawber I was always convinced that something would turn up. One afternoon I was lying in the bath and Mandy was sitting on the loo chatting, we were both having a good moan. Mandy was disillusioned about the club, she had expected to be swept off her feet by a peer of the realm, just like the old Gaiety Girl days, and it wasn't happening fast enough. We decided we were fed up with work, our Arabs, that we were tired and grossly underpaid.

I picked up on her mood quickly. I was always ready for a change of scene, I have always been impulsive and I began to concoct an escape from our routine immediately.

'Let's leave the club and get a flat together,' I prompted enthusiastically.

'But what can we do instead?' Mandy was the sensible one and worried about where her cash was coming from even before she needed to spend it – I lived from hour to hour and when I wanted to do something I wanted it NOW. Also I was convinced that if Murrays had taken me back once they would do so again. And there would always be Stephen if things went wrong.

'We will become models,' I announced confidently. 'Just one day's work a week and we'll earn as much as we get at the club. Oh, we'll be able to go out in the evenings . . . and have parties at the flat, it will be marvellous.'

28

Mandy was still doubtful but a little afraid of me at the time. 'What will we do about a down payment?' she asked. 'And in any case I owe four weeks' rent.'

'We'll borrow it from Michael, you know, that tall handsome chap from the club. He's always going on about my working there, I'll tell him he'll be able to see me every night, he'll be delighted.' I was in one of my wicked, ready-for-anything moods. 'And we'll do a moonlight flit from your place.'

I was right, Michael was delighted when I rang him to tell him we had found a flat in Comeragh Road in Barons Court and obligingly gave me fifty pounds; after all it was going to be cheaper than paying to see me at the club. This time, although I still couldn't tell Stephen to his face, I left him a note saying I was going to share with a girlfriend.

But first we had to arrange a moonlight flit for Mandy. We roped in a mystified Michael and got him to park his car just up the road. He wanted to know why we were moving at this time of night and we assured him it was just because we were so excited we couldn't wait. We crept in to get Mandy's belongings and were trying not to giggle as we crept down the stairs. But then Mandy dropped her teddy bear which fell bump, bump all the way down. The landlady heard us and caught us right in the act.

'And where do you think you are going, Miss Davies?' she demanded.

I scuttled out, leaving poor Mandy to face the music, and ran like a frightened rabbit to the car. I had to explain what we were up to to Michael, who was furious at being dragged into something so sordid. But then he was so rich he just couldn't understand people not paying their rent. We waited for ages and finally I begged Michael to go and find out what was happening.

'I'm staying well out of it,' he said firmly, thoroughly cross.

I decided to phone Mandy. I didn't fancy facing the landlady myself.

'She's threatened to call the police if I don't pay, she won't let me go.' Poor Mandy was nearly hysterical as she said this, so I went back to the car and collected another forty pounds off a very exasperated Michael and we were away.

Comeragh Road was wonderful. And the mischief we got into! We dressed ourselves in our best clothes and went to an expensive restaurant, ordered champagne and acted very grand. The bill came to thirteen pounds so Mandy whipped a petits-fours tray on the way out to make sure we'd got our money's worth. The other customers would have been very surprised to see those two elegant ladies on their way home, our legs dangling out of the taxi window, stuffing ourselves with sweets, pissed out of our little minds on champagne.

There was another time when some poor bloke called on us. For some reason or other he had offended us, I cannot remember what the grievance was, but we were ready for him when he called. We had both of us piddled in a bowl, added some water and when he rang the doorbell Mandy answered it and chucked the contents all over him. We were enjoying ourselves too much to bother about getting modelling work, since we had found a couple of Persian boyfriends who lived round the corner and took us out to the Whisky à Gogo a lot and I was always on the tap to Michael. He was getting thoroughly fed up with giving me money especially as he wasn't seeing as much of me as he had expected.

One morning we woke up broke again and realised we would have to pull a really fast one on Michael to get any more money from him. We decided on a nigh-unto-death-bed scene. I made up my face with talcum powder, Mandy devised a professional-looking medicine out of strawberry jam, and then she rang him to say I was desperately ill.

I lay back on the pillows doing my Camille act, looking all languid, and explained to Michael that I was in urgent need of seventy pounds for an operation. His refusal was instant, adamant and final: he told me he had handed out enough already. Furthermore he didn't believe my story and started to ask a lot of awkward questions like the name of my doctor and the nature of the op. This was Mandy's cue to bustle in with the medicine which I made a pathetic fuss about taking. We got our seventy quid and I fell into a deep untroubled sleep with relief and gratitude while Michael tip-toed from the flat. The door had barely clicked shut before I was out of bed getting dressed and made up. Our Persian boyfriends were due round at any minute, it had been a close thing. Poor Michael, I didn't mean to be heartless but I was too young to take anyone or anything seriously.

Inevitably the day came when we had to start taking money seriously and find a way of earning it for ourselves. Equally inevitably we took the easy way out again. A friend of ours, Nina Gadd, who was what was then called 'a girl about town', introduced us to the 21 Club in Mayfair and told us of the set-up there. As at Murrays, discretion was the password. All we had to do was look glamorous – which was easy with the help of Peter Rachman's clothes – and we would be invited to join the gentlemen members for drinks or dinner. It was all very civilised, the place was run like a continuous party and as we knew one or two of the girls there it was both fun and, through the grapevine in the ladies, safe. Again, like Murrays, there was never any pressure to oblige, but there were rooms available upstairs and we frequently accompanied a gentleman or two to his room. The place was a high-class knocking shop really, though the club never took any money off us; they supplied the goods and we kept what we earned.

Money was never discussed beforehand – nothing so vulgar – but Mandy was always a mercenary little thing and somehow she would extract more money from them. A murmur of rent overdue, a laddered stocking, or hoping to visit mum at the weekend – and their wallets would empty. We egged each other on in boldness and became experts at threesomes, though there was never any lesbianism in our act. Anyhow that sort of man was so knocked out with having one girl sit on his face while the other sucked his cock that he wasn't interested in exhibitionism. They were definitely getting a treat they couldn't get at home as we were both utterly uninhibited. The funny thing is, neither of us felt the slightest moral qualm. Screwing was fun in any case and it seemed a great way to get our playtime money which we spent on clothes, make-up, taxis and going to discos. We were enjoying life and once had a jolly threesome with Douglas Fairbanks Jnr just for the hell of it. It was larky to be balling a famous film star and for him our services were free.

It was at the 21 Club that I met my very sweet 'money man', Major Eylan, who was to become a regular client over two years, visiting me at Comeragh Road and later at Stephen's house in Wimpole Mews. He became my regular source of income and it was because I spent some of this money on household expenses that the courts were eventually able to get Stephen for living off immoral earnings.

But that was all in the future. At that time I was just a wild, carefree girl using my assets to have a good time. It never occurred to me that I would one day be called a prostitute and whore because those words only applied to the girls who stood on street corners soliciting strangers.

It was while we were living at Comeragh Road that I first met Lord 'Bill' Astor. Although I had often been to the cottage at Cliveden with Stephen I had never been to the big house, though Stephen was often asked up there to sort out a guest's ailments or Bill's bad back and would sometimes be asked to stay on for drinks or dinner. I remember him telling me about one occasion when he was invited to stay on. One of the other guests was an American, something important in the car industry. There must have been some political deal going on because he didn't fit in with the country-seat scene at all, and certainly didn't know the rules of the English dinner table; after the first course he lit up a cigarette. Lord Astor asked him very politely to stub it out. The American protested.

'But I like smoking.'

'And I like fucking,' snapped his lordship, 'but I do not do it at the dinner table.' And that was that, no smoking allowed until the ladies had left the table. Stephen was laughing all the time he told the story, the American was so confused. He couldn't understand how, with ladies present, smoking could be taboo but the rich use of the Anglo-Saxon acceptable. Stephen was also feeling very smug as he was a chain smoker and had had to control his own longing for a cigarette. Innate good manners were part of Stephen's charm and he acknowledged that, however casual was his relationship with Bill in London, at Cliveden the conventions must be observed. There was never any question of his orgiastic, voyeurist games or friends being introduced to the big house, and consequently neither Mandy nor myself were ever guests at the formal dinner parties despite what has been written elsewhere. Indeed Mandy only went to the cottage about three times because Stephen didn't like her very much.

I had called Stephen one afternoon, our Persian boyfriends had gone on holiday so we were at a loose end.

'Where have you been, you naughty little baby?' he asked. It was exciting to hear his voice again and I realised how much I had missed him and how much I had to tell him.

'Oh, Stephen, I'm having such a wonderful time, I'm living with a girl friend and I'm sure you'll like her, please come round to see us.'

So Stephen started popping in, often bringing friends with him. One day he brought his cousin, Tim Vigors, a Battle of Britain pilot who was badly scarred and for a short while I thought I was in love with this brave and gallant man. I knew he was crazy about me, he was very romantic and liked to wander around holding hands. It was all very idyllic until the day he announced that his divorce had come through and he could now live with me for good. I got cold feet instantly and turned to Mandy who was always quick to devise a plan to get out of trouble. I had foolishly given him a key to the flat so we couldn't just pretend to be out. We were busy composing a regretful note saying I had changed my mind, I was too young to settle down yet and would he please leave the key, when we heard his car draw up outside. We flung the note on the table and raced into the spare room to hide under the bed, our hands clapped over our mouths to stifle the giggles. Rotten little sods, we waited till he had gone then sailed off to celebrate our lovely irresponsible freedom. Stephen was cross with us because we had hurt Tim (though I daresay Tim was grateful later) but I defended myself saying that he was old enough to know better. I had yet to experience that sort of pain myself.

Because I had heard so much about him from Stephen I wasn't in the least bit overwhelmed at meeting Bill Astor. He was a lot of fun, he got very randy when he'd had a few drinks and spent the evening trying to pinch our bottoms, but he got a bit irritable when he saw he wasn't getting anywhere with either of us. I don't know why we didn't, particularly Mandy as she dearly loved a title. Perhaps we thought it would make things difficult for Stephen at Cliveden, maybe we just thought of him as a friend. He was certainly a visitor but it was always for laughs and he was a good enough friend to turn to when we were short of the next quarter's rent. Mandy asked him if we could borrow £200 and he wrote out a cheque immediately. Mandy was to repay him later by screwing him and then by accepting £500 from the *Daily Express* to mention his name in court. She was paid the same sum by Savundra to keep his out. Perhaps another reason on my part for not going to bed with Bill is that I have always liked forceful men, those who knew what they wanted (me) and were determined to get it. Jack Profumo, Major Eylan and Peter Rachman all came into that category, they were strong, commanders of the situation. Being a passive person I was happier in the company of decision-makers, a character defect I have paid for highly since then, both financially and emotionally. I wounded my imploring lovers because they didn't have the strength to take me, it was as simple as that.

Every now and again we made sporadic attempts on our modelling careers, with Mandy being far the more ambitious and resourceful of the two of us. Modelling was fast replacing becoming an air hostess as *the* glamour job for girls who wanted to get on in life; commercial television was beginning to realise that pretty girls could sell products and there were still plenty of roles in films for aspiring actresses, otherwise known as nice bits of crumpet. Stardom could only be just round the corner.

We decided not to wait, we'd go seek it out. We had listened to enough conversations among rich and powerful businessmen around the West End to know where the action was. We had conquered London. The South of France was about to get its turn. As ever, it all had to be done on the spur of the moment, which wasn't easy in the days before the tourist boom and with the economic restrictions of 1961. Travellers' cheques took weeks to organise and each person was allowed to take only £20 out of the country. Our first move was to make a raid on Knightsbridge buying up everything we could possibly need, summer clothes, shampoo, toothpaste, flourishing cheques we knew were going to bounce all the way from the bank. We didn't care, we were going to be rich and famous.

First stop was Paris and a small hotel in St Germain, then sauntering round the tourist spots dressed to kill. I had the clothes and Mandy had the hats. We had been there about four days before we ran out of money and began to wonder how the hell we were going to get to the South of France. It was time to stop concentrating on the monuments and start looking for providers. We found them in Notre Dame, two good-looking Spaniards who were also more interested in the beauties of the present than the historical building. It was an easy pick-up and we willingly accepted the offer of a lift back to our hotel in their hired car and a night out at the Lido.

Back in the hotel we hatched our plan. They had a car, we wanted to head south. The car was hired so it wasn't the same as stealing, all we had to do was get hold of the keys. That was Mandy's job, for she had more nerve than I did. I would do the driving.

So it was on with best bib and tucker, sweetest smiles, and keep a careful watch where he put the keys, which were attached to a rather large rubber ball. Luckily for us this was before the days of skintight pants, though Mandy had quite a job getting them from his back pocket. Very flirtatious we both had to be, with me manoeuvring my partner away from the scene of the crime with the usual unspoken promises of the pleasures to come. A triumphant glance from Mandy told me all was well and it was time for a trip to the ladies' and out the side exit. We had to move quickly to get to our hotel before our escorts missed us and the keys, and we had to be out of the place before they grabbed a cab and caught us. Of course the damn car wouldn't start, it was a left-hand drive model and I didn't know how to work the lights. We were really beginning to panic when we saw a gendarme heading towards us. Two pretty faces peered up at him helplessly and his national gallantry came to our rescue. He showed me the switches, gave us a push and wished us 'bon voyage.' We shot round to the hotel, grabbed our things and aimed ourselves out of Paris. It wasn't easy because neither of us had thought to buy a map, but then nothing on that journey was easy. We were somewhere in the middle of France when we noticed the petrol gauge was very low but not half as low as our funds which were non-existent.

'I'll deal with it,' said Mandy. 'You get the car filled and have the engine running while I explain.'

Her 'explanation' was a useless English cheque which she handed to the astounded attendant. We were half a mile down the road before the poor man recovered his wits. The car eventually cracked up altogether and we had to hitch, quite a hazardous venture though we were more frightened of being robbed of our suitcases than we were of being raped. We finally got to Cannes with a lift from a young naval officer. Tired, hungry, dirty and broke, we fell into a cheap hotel in the middle of the night.

The morning sunshine and sparkling sea soon restored our spirits, but one thing was certain – we had to get hold of some money fast. Explaining to the porter that we needed some francs to get to the bank, we set off. But not for the bank – to the grand hotels along the seafront, where the porter's francs went on a couple of cokes to sip while we sussed out the scene.

Our luck was in, and strolling along the front came a film producer who Mandy had met at the 21 Club. I can't remember if he been a client or not, but he soon got the message. Mandy made it very clear that we were available on a strictly cash basis.

It suited him fine as it always does with the kind of men who prefer to pay for sex. Flaunting a couple of dolly birds enhances their virile image and they are quite happy to go along with the pretence that they are helping you with your career, introducing you to wealthy people and places and a life-style far removed from the average girl's origins. It seemed like a fair enough exchange: the good life amongst powerful men talking big money deals, every tab being picked up by one of them, bedding one of them in their grand hotels during siesta time, going out with young men during the evening and all that sunshine too. It has been said that we made our money at the casinos but that's not true; it couldn't have been, because the French were very strict about minors being able to gamble. When we tried to get in once our passports were demanded for inspection and as we were both under age, we were refused entry.

Nevertheless we returned to London richer than we went away, with enough money to fly back and for me to buy mum a brand new bicycle. Mandy and I decided to throw a little party to show off our tans. I invited Peter Rachman because I hadn't seen him since we had broken up and, in a sudden rush of generosity, I remembered how good he had been to me. Stephen came too, which brought a slight atmosphere of hostility as Stephen had never forgiven Peter for taking me away from him, and neither did he approve of Peter's attitude to money or women. So it fell to Mandy to entertain Peter and I could see they hit it off right away. She was just the type of girl Peter needed, a pretty face, a bit of a bird brain and very happy to be looked after and sheltered. He was perfect for her, his money and generosity impressed her and very soon she was moving into the Bryanston Mews flat that I had shared with Peter and Cherie. Our Comeragh Road days were over.

I moved my belongings back to Stephen's spare room, happy to be home again and to be amongst his constant stream of visitors, but now I was also going through my very first painful love affair. Manu, the rich Persian student for whom I had dumped both Michael Lambton and Tim Vigors, had come back from his holiday, and I was crazy about him. The tables were well and truly turned on me. I was used to men running after me, being anxious to please, paying me a lot of attention. This one walloped me if I stepped out of line and because he played on my jealousy I was always making big scenes. I was furious to find a man who had just the same attitude to women that I had to men. I couldn't understand how he didn't want to be with me all the time. He had a room in a hostel in Horseferry Road where I wasn't supposed to stay but I did because I never brought boyfriends back to Stephen's house, at least at night.

'I'm going out tonight,' he would announce, and I knew that meant he would come back drunk in the early hours of the morning. I hated waiting up for him but I couldn't help myself. Sometimes I would chase round the clubs in the West End searching for him and when he saw me he'd just go on talking and laughing with his friends and ignore me. I'd get desperate and clutch at his sleeve, begging him to come home, make the sort of scenes that can still make me shudder at the memory. I suppose most people have gone through the torments of jealousy but it is absolute hell when you are living it. Stephen kept trying to persuade me to forget all about Manu but nevertheless he found him useful too.

Three times he asked me to deliver letters to Eugene Ivanov at the Russian Embassy, saying they were invitations to a bridge party or apologies for not being able to make it. Each time it was Manu who drove me there and it was only later when he reported this fact to the police that I realised the packages were too bulky to be scribbled notes.

Our affair didn't last very long. He was sadistic, dominant, and loved to see me cringe before his threats but still it wasn't enough; when he told me to go I thought my heart would break. I told Stephen all about it and he very sensibly drove me to Horseferry Road, insisting that I pick up my things while he waited for me to make sure I didn't weaken.

I didn't have the chance. When I got there Manu was sitting on his bed showing his new girlfriend photographs. I screamed and hit him, hard, and ran to the comfort of Stephen's arms.

'There, there, little baby, you are safe now. We'll go home and make some coffee and watch TV.' I was never going to leave him again.

CHAPTER THREE

STEPHEN WARD was not just a highly successful osteopath, a manipulator of bones, he was a great manipulator of people's minds too.

For some he was a passport to splendour and riches: people like Bronwen Pugh, Maureen Swanson and Maggie Brown all married brilliantly through Stephen's introductions. He always said I should have been a duchess but his influence on my life was less fortunate, as the world now knows. Not that I blame him for all my misfortunes. He tried very hard to teach me not to accept money from men in exchange for sex. He didn't approve of my taking the easy way out and genuinely wanted me to be successful at first. He believed in women being independent, making their own way in life, he was all for equality and often said that women were more intelligent, more possessed of their faculties than most men whom he usually described as 'dirty bastards just following their pricks.'

I was the last of a long run of girls whom Stephen had cultivated, escorted and encouraged; my misfortune was that Stephen's time was running out.

I was 17 and he was 46 when we met. He was charming, funny and outrageous. He was well-known both as an osteopath and as an artist, he was welcomed everywhere, at grand houses, dinner parties, embassies. He had been commissioned by the *Illustrated London News* to do no less than nine portraits of the Royal Family, including Prince

Philip, whom he had known before he married the Princess Elizabeth. He should have been heading for greatness, perhaps even some kind of official recognition. But he wasn't, he was heading for disgrace and death.

Stephen committed the one cardinal sin; that of lacking discretion. He was the most almighty gossip and name-dropper and, with access to a London seething with sexuality behind very posh portals, his knowledge of upper-class frailties must have been dangerous, though he wouldn't have known it. He was a mischief-maker because he could not take anyone or anything seriously. The fact that the people he saw at orgies screwing in all directions were the bastions of Britain's law and order society only made him crease with laughter. Remember that at that time Britain took the prostitutes off the streets and refused to acknowledge the existence of homosexuality as natural between some men. Divorce was still shameful and the class delineation was still very strong. Britain was hypocritical and Stephen knew it; what he didn't know was that he would be the catalyst who would blow it wide open.

Kinky was the word that came out of the Stephen Ward set and, in what would now seem to be a very modest way, he was. He kept high-heeled shoes, stockings and suspenders in his wardrobe, not because he was a transvestite but because those were the garments that turned him on when a girlfriend wore them. He didn't need a lot of sex – once a fortnight was about his average – but he lived for other people's sex lives. He would wait up for me wanting to know every detail of my night and then tell me every detail of his (there must be a lot of people around who are thankful that I have a memory like a sieve; he remembererd every name). We would giggle into the night as he told me about the orgy he had just come from where the barristers, having finished their part of the game, would stand around talking about the prosecution of obscene books. *Lady Chatterley's Lover* had just been published as a test case, but in comparison some of the pornographic books these eminent City men passed around made *Lady Chatterley* look like a fairy story for the under-sevens.

Much as Stephen liked to talk about other people, he very seldom spoke of his own past, though he would talk about the women who had lived with him in Devonshire Street – Maureen Swanson, and Vickie Martin who had been killed in a car crash before I came on the scene. But never of his childhood or the war, perhaps because he thought it would bore me or maybe talking of the past made him feel old. I did not know at the time that he had been invalided out of the services for 'nerves', but I do remember we were at a party once and a man accused him of having been a coward. I could see Stephen was livid but he didn't say a word and we left the party immediately. Though his father was a vicar, it is obvious that his influence was slight as Stephen had no belief in God. His code of life was pagan, if anything, on a personal level and socialist on a political level. And looking back I suppose it was his paganism, his do-as-you-please attitude to life, that gave him so much influence over so many people, including myself. He was kind to the point of being over-indulgent with friends. They would seek him out to discuss their problems and he would encourage them to do what they secretly wanted to, particularly if they wanted to flout the rules of society. That was why he would give a model's phone number to a War Minister, for instance – the excitement of scandal in high places was irresistible.

He was a strange man but not queer, not homosexual at all. I think he couldn't actually come and I should know because he would call me in to watch while he was on the job. Looking back we had a weird relationship; he only once made a half-hearted attempt at making love to me but neither of us were very interested and he let it go with a laugh as usual. He liked to cuddle and touch, he was a very sensual person and so am I, we slept together most of the time throughout our living together. When he brought a bird back to the flat he would always call me to his bedroom and make me listen to an elaborate running commentary. I would stand there for a while then wander off leaving the door open so he knew I was around. He couldn't bear to sleep the night with a girl he had screwed and insisted that I slept beside him, between them.

He had one girlfriend, Valerie, who liked to be tied up and whipped. This amused him enormously until she went off and married a barrister who was a real sadist, whereupon he turned very vicious and bitchy and tried to get the information published. Yet he was very sweet to me, too sweet in fact. When I finally got a model's portfolio together and started to get work I would say to him, 'Oh, I don't feel like doing it today' and he would tell me not to bother, we would go for a drive or a coffee instead. I've never been a great one for getting up so I never left the fold, he wanted us to stay together, and I would do anything he told me. We were very much partners at the time, when we went out together we always held hands but if Stephen fancied some girl he would whisper to me that he wanted her and it was my job to procure her attention. It just seemed like drawing somebody into the conversation at the time but I was definitely his little piece of bait. It's funny to think that at the same time up-market hostesses were wandering around Buckingham Palace garden parties with pretty much the same job in mind.

I did meet one man through Stephen, that was Charles who lived in Green Street and who gave me money. Stephen had brought him round from the surgery and threw us quite deliberately together. All the time, of course, I had my dear Major Eylan who would come round occasionally and when it was my turn to spend on the household goods or a cab that was where the money came from. I was living rent free but that was never taken into account when the accusations were made.

There were still many others coming to the house, like Alfred Marks the actor and his wife, and Lord d'Lazlo, who were fun, and Sir Godfrey Nicholson or Eugene Ivanov who always had serious conversations with Stephen that bored me.

Stephen was also beginning to get bored with the orgy set and visited them less frequently; he was restless and looking for new thrills, new enthusiasms. We started going for late-night drives round the back of Paddington to spot the prostitutes working. It seemed that everyone was working the street, Westbourne Grove, from a local launderette. We'd sit in the car and watch a handsome black girl stroll along till she got there, whereupon a big black man would emerge from the doorway and the girl would pull out a wad of notes and hand them over. She got a grin, a nod of approval for her pains and an indication to get out there and earn some more. We followed, fascinated and a bit nervous, for though it was fun it was scary too.

Suddenly a really hideous old hag pushed her head through the broken basement railings. 'Fuck off you black bastard!' she screamed.

Our girl sneered and twitched her hips even more deliberately. She knew who would get first pickings if there were any to be had. Stephen was giggling helplessly at the sight of the old battered black woman, covered in white make-up to pass as lighter.

'God, do you think she's like that all over? Go on, Christine, go up and ask her if she is withered all over,' he urged.

At that time I'd do almost anything for Stephen to give him a kick but the very thought of approaching someone so patently bug-ridden made me shudder. The girl was

45

approached by a little mackintoshed man with thick specs but although he thrust a couple of quid under her nose she wasn't having any. Then she spotted a large Irish-looking man across the road and she was away, though he didn't seem all that interested.

'Bet you ten bob she doesn't make him,' said Stephen, totally enthralled. It was better than the theatre. He lost the bet, they went off together.

'Why don't you have a go?' Stephen was laughing as he said it.

'Don't be crazy. Walk down this street on my own?'

'I don't mean seriously. Look, we'll pick a road in Notting Hill Gate where there is a milk machine, then you just walk along and see how many men try to pick you up. We'll have a bet on it.'

It shows how serious Stephen was that he gave me the sixpence for the machine. He parked about a hundred yards away and I set off for the machine very nervously. Two or three cars slowed down but I just kept marching on, head high. On the way back a small Asian tried to offer for me and by the time I neared the car I was practically running. I could see Stephen sitting in the car falling about with laughter, I heard someone behind me call, 'Hello darling', and as I got to the door I felt a hand on my shoulder. I was terrified but Stephen was very excited and two nights later he brought a prostitute home. I wasn't asked to share this experience and from then on I kept my bedroom door locked whenever he brought one back with him. Stephen was beginning to change.

It was typical of Stephen to explore the back areas of West London at this time; there was a lot of racial tension around, violence in the streets and a lot of prejudice from the middle-class whites. Stephen liked to be first in the field – it was a new topic to talk about, to relate first-hand to his smart friends. It was also typical that he insisted I accompany him because he knew I had recently had an extraordinary experience at Wimpole Mews.

I was alone in the flat one day when I felt a presence in the room. There, standing behind me, was an enormous black man with a big beard, wearing a leopard skin and holding a devil's fork. I was petrified, I knew it was a ghost and I ran to the bathroom and locked myself in. Stephen found me hours later shivering with fear. It appeared again and again and each time I felt terribly threatened. Stephen even brought a hypnotist round to get this man out of my thoughts but he couldn't hypnotise me. I see it now as a premonition of the disasters ahead of me, though others might see it as an unconscious fixation with blacks.

Certainly the man who took my virginity was from Ghana. He was a sweeper at the shop where I had my first job modelling. He told me that he was a student and asked me to help him with his studies. I went to his room one Saturday afternoon and all he wanted to do was talk about how lonely he was, how much he needed a friend. He wanted to kiss me and I let him, then he wanted me to get into bed with him and I said I had to go.

'But we won't do it properly,' he explained. 'Just hold each other, if we don't do it properly it can't do any harm.'

I was curious to find out what it would be like so I agreed, and of course once he had started he went the whole way. I was not very stimulated by the experience – quite a lot of people say the same thing about their first time – but once it had happened I began to feel that I didn't have very much to lose. I never saw him again but on the train home I began to feel guilty and full of secret shame for what I had done.

Curiously it was the nuns at the convent that I was sent to at the age of nine who introduced me to the existence of blacks as people. I suppose like any child of the time I must have seen pictures of natives in the bush in my geography lessons but they used to tell us for our bedtime story an old

47

fable about Rastus, a little black boy, and his love for a little white girl. One day the little girl was taken to hospital and Rastus was told that she would die before the leaves on the tree outside her window fell. He climbed the tree and tied all the leaves on with shoelaces. One night along came a great wind that took away the leaves and the little girl died.

I suppose they were trying to imbue us with love for our fellow men and the uselessness of not accepting God's will but the effect on me must have been very deep. Romantic love and the inevitability of death are a strong diet for an already sensitive and wayward child.

It was still difficult to assess whether Stephen's intentions, as we moved deeper and deeper into Paddington and Notting Hill, were to cure me, to solve some hidden problem or whether once again he was encouraging me to act out what he thought were my secret fantasies. We started going regularly to a seedy restaurant full of West Indians and Stephen would sit for hours happily drawing the new, unusual faces around him. Stephen was as adaptable as a chameleon and could talk to anyone from a down-and-out to a duke, from an ex-convict to a count, and he was thrilled with his new scene where there was a fight outside the restaurant most nights and the police sirens and ambulances were never far away.

As usual he was incapable of finding new places and new people, of discovering different connections, without boasting about it to everyone. If people took up half of Stephen's life, telling others stories about the people he knew took up the other half.

Soon after our visits to the West Indian restaurant he was showing off to Lord d'Lazlo, relating the excitement of life in the raw.

'Come on,' he urged. 'Come and see it for yourself. Come and see that low life you're always reading about. No use talking about the problems of racialism if you don't know what goes on.'

His enthusiasm was infectious and we all piled into the car anticipating an evening of excitement like downtown Chicago in the movies. Our usual restaurant was a let down, practically empty. This wouldn't do, for if we disappointed d'Lazlo Stephen's reputation would be ruined. We had noticed an even seedier-looking place up the road so we moved on there. The new restaurant didn't know us and everyone in it was black. They looked at us with a kind of indifferent hostility but ignored us. We sat down and ordered some coffee but it was all rather boring, nothing to show off at all. A strange musty smell hung over the room.

'I think they are smoking pot, I can smell it,' Stephen whispered.

D'Lazlo and I were immediately interested. We had heard about pot but neither of us had ever tried it.

'What's it like?'

'I shouldn't think it has much effect, it probably depends on your attitude to it.' He glanced around at one or two of the glazed faces. 'I wonder if they sell it here.'

'Well, they certainly wouldn't sell it to us, they'd imagine us to be the law.' You could tell by Lord d'Lazlo's voice that he was fed up with Stephen's idea of an evening out slumming and if our adventure was to be rescued I had better do something fast. My anxiety to please Stephen made me daring.

'Why don't I see if I can get some,' I ventured.

'OK little baby, why not? We'll wait for you out in the car.'

'What do I ask for?'

'Grass or weed.'

With some trepidation I headed for the toilets, where I found a dark West Indian lounging against the passage wall.

'Hi there, baby, going some place?' he drawled without budging. He was blocking the passage to the loo. I stood there looking at him for a moment; he had an open neck shirt, not much hair but a neat beard and a moustache.

'I'm looking for someone,' I explained.

'Well, how about you an' me tonight?' He opened his mouth a little and ran his tongue over his teeth, making me very nervous.

'My friends are upstairs waiting for me . . . I'm looking for someone to sell me some weed,' I stuttered. He looked a bit taken aback – which isn't surprising, since there weren't too many well-dressed white girls floating round that manor in any case, let alone asking for supplies.

'How much?' was all he asked, still without moving.

'How does it come?' I didn't like showing my naivety but I had no choice.

'Pound, ten shill.' One eyebrow raised acknowledged his superiority.

'I'll take the ten shillings' worth.' I offered him a ten bob note, I was eager to be away.

He disappeared down the stairs, returning a few minutes later with a scruffy piece of paper. Inside there was a tiny amount of grassy looking stuff. I wondered if I'd been had.

'Going now, baby?' He had carefully positioned himself to block my exit.

'My brother's waiting, I've got to go home.'

He asked me if I would be returning tomorrow or sometime and instead of shaking my head I had a brilliant, and forever-to-be-regretted inspiration.

Stephen had for some time been hung up on the idea of screwing a black girl. While sketching them he would talk about their bone structure and skin texture. As ever, he had looked to me to find him one and we had joked about a great big, fat mama of a girl that I said I was going to pull for him. I had jumped up, pretending to be serious. He grabbed my arm, laughing and protesting at the same time. 'No, no, little baby, I'd never be able to find where to put it

50

in,' he had said. But he was serious, he did want a black girl and this was my chance to get him one.

'Yes,' I said cautiously, 'we might be able to meet again. The thing is . . . have you got a sister for my brother?'

'Sure thing, baby, plenty of them,' he smiled. 'Tomorrow then?'

'I don't know about tomorrow, look, I'll give you my telephone number and you can ring us when you've fixed one up.'

I rushed up the stairs, very proud of my success, and handed Stephen the grass. 'Guess what, Stephen, the man who sold it to me says he'll fix you up with one of his sisters; you've always said you wondered if it was any different, now you'll be able to find out.'

'Little baby, you are great. How did you manage that?' He turned to d'Lazlo. 'Don't you think she's fantastic, she finds girls for me. Are you sure you wouldn't like to rent her for a week? So when is it all happening?'

The evening had been turned around and we raced back to the flat full of merriment at the prospect of yet another new experience.

Afterwards Stephen and d'Lazlo gazed at me in pompous fashion, the joint had had no effect on them. But I was rolling about, it had really gone to my head and I was laughing and relaxed. But I would not have been so relaxed if I had known I had just met Lucky Gordon, the wild young black man who was indirectly to lead many of us to scandal and disgrace, some of us to imprisonment and Stephen to suicide. His inappropriate name was our doom.

Two days later Lucky rang to invite us to a party. His sister would be there, and we were to meet him first at the cafe.

'Stuff your money down the front of your dress,' Lucky warned me as we descended an ill-lit staircase to a damp, musty basement. What a freakout the place was. Most of the company was black apart from a couple of peroxide blondes and a few rather straight, civil-service type men. Beer was flowing from a barrel in the kitchen and black men were pissing straight into the sink. I think even Stephen was appalled, he couldn't bring himself to show any interest in his evening's date. Lucky had taken charge of me, proudly introducing me to everyone as 'his' girl, but there was too much noise from the music to talk to anyone, and in any case as soon as I smiled Lucky would drag me off to the next group. There was a lot of very vigorous dancing going on and a lot of pot being passed around. I couldn't take it, I soon felt my head going dizzy from the mixture of alcohol and cannabis. My legs went wobbly and I had to prop myself against a wall to stop myself floating into nothingness. I couldn't understand; I had been so larky and trigger-happy on dope back at the flat.

Stephen was quickly by my side, ordering Lucky to get me into the fresh air while he raced to get the car. Lucky carried me over his shoulder and as soon as the air hit me I recovered enough to stop Lucky's hand slipping down my bra after my money. I was struggling with him when Stephen arrived.

'She's not well, Lucky, let her go. I'm taking her home.'

'I'm taking her or I'll come with you.' Lucky was blocking the passenger door to our two-seater and still hanging on to me. The friction between the two men quickly brought me to my senses and I broke away and ran for the driver's side and clambered into the safety of the car. Lucky was still shouting about taking me home so I called through the window that I would be all right.

'See you around then, Lucky,' said Stephen amiably. He had no wish for a fight, nor did he want to lose contact with Lucky and his friends, since he had just made arrangements with a dope peddler in case any of his friends wanted some pot. It was just becoming the fashionable, daring thing to do.

From that moment on Lucky was seldom off the phone, and we both got fed up with dreaming up excuses for me not to see him. Even our guests would join in the chorus of 'That's Lucky' when the phone rang because Stephen had not been slow to report that we had been to a ghetto party and that a black man had fallen in love with Christine.

Endlessly I told him I was busy, that I was engaged to someone, that I wasn't feeling well, and each time the calls would end up accusing me of not wanting to see him because he was black, which I would hotly deny. Of course it was the truth; it was all very well to go slumming with Stephen and his friends but to walk down the street on your own with a black was unthinkable. People would look. And besides my mother would have a fit if she ever found out that I had even spoken to one. I felt rotten about it, I could see it was terribly unfair. Perhaps that little Rastus fable was at work because one day I gave in. Reluctantly admittedly, but I thought having a coffee with him would stop him feeling rejected because of his colour. Even so I arranged to meet him somewhere where I wouldn't run into anybody I knew.

Over coffee he told me he wanted to show me something back at his place.

'It's some jewellery. I want to get rid of it and I thought you might be able to help me. Please, Christine.'

Amongst the many places Stephen and I went to looking for excitement or the hint of danger was a hoods' club, full of charming villains who accepted us as friends. We knew a lot of 'exchange and mart' went on, so maybe I could help him. We walked up hundreds of stairs, Lucky behind me, urging me to keep going. He opened the door to his flat and told me to keep going. I did as I was told and found myself in a bedroom. I turned to say 'Where's the jewellery?' but the words never got past my lips. He was standing there, leaning against the door with a knife in his hand.

My mind went utterly blank. Not until much later did the

terrifying stories of murdered girls found dumped on wastelands occur to me. I looked into his eyes which had turned into those of a madman, both glowing and cold, squinting almost as if he couldn't see me. He came towards me and I found my voice.

'Don't be silly, Lucky. Where are these jewels you were talking about?' He didn't answer.

'I think I had perhaps better be going home.' He still didn't respond, but flicked the knife as I made towards the door.

'Take off your dress.' He was already unbuttoning his shirt with his left hand. The first thing that came to my mind was that he would rip my dress off with the knife if I didn't obey. I took it off. Holding the knife at my throat he forced me on to the bed and tore my knickers off. Every time I struggled or tried to reason with him he became more excited; I could see that because by now he had his trousers off displaying an enormous erection. I could see there was no arguing with that. Afterwards I felt disgusted, violated, and I knew that a lot of my disgust came from the fact that he was black. I said nothing, didn't scream 'Rape' or anything silly, just crossed the room to pick up my dress.

'You're staying here,' he shouted, looking nasty again.

'What do you mean staying here? You've lied to me and had what you wanted and I have to go home now.' He didn't look half as frightening without his erection, in fact he looked a bit pathetic standing naked with a knife in his hand.

'You're not going to kill me with that silly little knife, are you?' I was feeling bolder now it was over and the knife didn't look as threatening either.

He went out of the room, locking it behind him. I searched desperately around but there was no means of escape. The windows were sealed and we were too high to contemplate climbing out the window. The telephone, if he

54

had one, must have been in the other room.

Lucky was back in seconds and I quickly covered myself with one of the dirty grey blankets on his bed – he didn't even have sheets and the room smelt stale.

'Uncover yourself,' he ordered. I tightened the blanket round my throat. Lucky started to play gently with the knife, throwing it skilfully from hand to hand, and I could see he was getting excited again. Not so soon, I thought. Surely you don't want it again so soon.

'Why are you keeping me here? What are you going to do with me?' I couldn't keep the fear out of my voice now and this was what he was waiting for. His movements were slow and deliberate. He caught the edge of the blanket with the knife and flicked it on to the floor, leaving me naked again. I felt mesmerised by the knife and his eyes and I preferred to watch the knife. I was frightened that if he saw my hatred and contempt he would surely kill me. My survival depended on behaving meekly; he needed to feel he possessed me utterly and completely.

Once again he threw himself on me like the maniac he was, pumping himself into me like a machine. I knew resistance would make him both angry and more excited so I lay there passively, waiting for his monotonous energy to subside. When he was finished I asked him once again to let me go. He was quite shocked.

'Didn't you enjoy it?'

'No,' I replied truthfully. It was the wrong answer.

'But look, I love you, we could be happy together surely?'

I smiled and agreed that maybe we could but it was too early, while all of me wanted to scream 'I hate you, I hate you, let me go, you filthy animal'. By now I had realised the real danger I was in, that the little knife in that man's hands was capable of cutting my throat and spilling my entrails on the floor. I pleaded to telephone Stephen, just to let him know where I was. It was dark outside by now and I had lost track of the time since I had met Lucky at six. He turned away from me and went to sleep with one hand gripping my arm. Every time I moved his muscles tensed. I was wide awake, trying to plan an escape. I gazed longingly at my dress on the floor and waited for his breathing to become rhythmic and even. Slowly I put one foot out of bed but as my toe reached the cold, dirty linoleum he sat bolt upright and clamped me down with his arm.

I wanted to cry but I couldn't, so finally I slept out of sheer nervous exhaustion. My ordeal began again the next day. I was painfully sore from my battering and started to cry which added greatly to his enjoyment. I even had to beg to go to the lavatory and he stood outside all the time. I was in despair, but now it was time to try new tactics. It seemed like everything I did turned him on. If I struggled he got violently excited, if I played meek and mild he took longer to enjoy himself. I had to try being sensible.

'Look, Lucky, by now Stephen will be very worried. I have never stayed away from him so long. He knew I was going to meet you and if I don't ring him soon he will be contacting the police and directing them to the cafe you go to. They will have to tell the police where you live.'

Thank God that at that moment I did not know that the man I was talking to, Aloysius 'Lucky' Gordon had numerous previous convictions for larceny, rape, and grievous bodily harm, one of the latter consisting of sticking a knife up a girl's vagina. I would doubtless have threatened him and been dead seconds later. As it was I put my arms round him affectionately to show him my concern was only for Stephen's peace of mind.

He agreed that I could phone Stephen, but first . . . then he was off again.

Finally he brought the phone in from his friend's room next door. I caught Stephen in his office, hoping that he would hear my desperation across the wires. He did and began to shout angrily down the phone.

'I've been worried sick about you, you naughty little baby. How dare you behave like this. If you are not home in half an hour I am coming to get you.'

Lucky had been listening but was still reluctant to let me go.

'But I must,' I explained. 'Stephen is very snobbish and could make a lot of trouble. He wouldn't understand that you love me, he doesn't understand coloured people.' It was unfair to blame Stephen but any story would do to get me away, so I went on. 'Of course I didn't understand at first. Naturally I was frightened of you. You see English girls are brought up to think of coloured men as bogeymen, something evil, but now I know better.'

My patent lies mollified him a bit and after making many promises to see him again soon I unobtrusively got into my dress and managed to act out a sad farewell. I walked slowly down the stairs, truly heart in mouth, and when I got to the corner of the street I ran like hell till I found a cab.

Stephen was there to hold me tight when I got back and for once he didn't laugh as I poured out my 18-hour ordeal. He sat beside me as I wallowed in a hot, cleansing, soothing bath.

'Poor little baby. You are home and safe now, I think we will just have to forget this one, there's no point in taking proceedings; it would be very sordid and we could have the entire population of Paddington rise up against us. Besides, darling,' he pointed out to try and cheer me up, 'it could actually have been worse, there could have been six of them, I hear they go in for gang bangs quite a bit.'

If either of us had known what we were to find out about Lucky Gordon some months later I don't think even Stephen would have been quite so sanguine. As it was I just crept into bed and slept for twenty-four hours.

The nuisance phone calls continued and were particularly incessant one afternoon when Sir Oswald Mosley was present. After a while he became curious about the performance of the phone ringing and Stephen and I taking it in turns to slam the phone down. For once Stephen was evasive.

'Someone worrying Christine,' was all he said.

Sir Oswald had not been gone many minutes before the doorbell rang. I looked out of the window.

'Oh, my God, Stephen, it's him, there are two of them.'

'Thank heavens Sir Oswald has gone, they'd have skinned him alive if they recognised him, he is definitely not their favourite person, he can't stand blacks. Look, Christine, we are going to have to face this out. I've had enough of this pestering. You are going to tell him in front of me that you do not want anything more to do with him. Anyone in their right mind will see that they must stop this sort of behaviour.'

What neither of us realised was that he was not in his right mind. As I went down the stairs, not entirely convinced of the wisdom of Stephen's counsel, I wondered how he had found our address. When I opened the door Lucky's companion was the man Stephen had met at the party, the dope supplier that Stephen wanted to keep in with.

'All I want to do is have a word with her in private,' announced Lucky as he entered the room.

'You can talk in here,' said Stephen severely, very much king of his castle, but somehow Lucky managed to convey that he was intent on apologising and it had to be done in private. Feeling safe because Stephen was there, I followed him into the bedroom. His mood changed immediately. He locked the door behind us and flung me on to the bed. This time I was able to scream before his hand clamped over my mouth and Stephen was banging on the door yelling that he

58

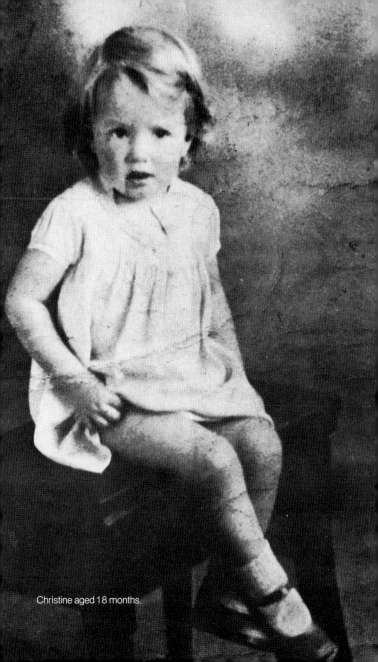
Christine aged 18 months.

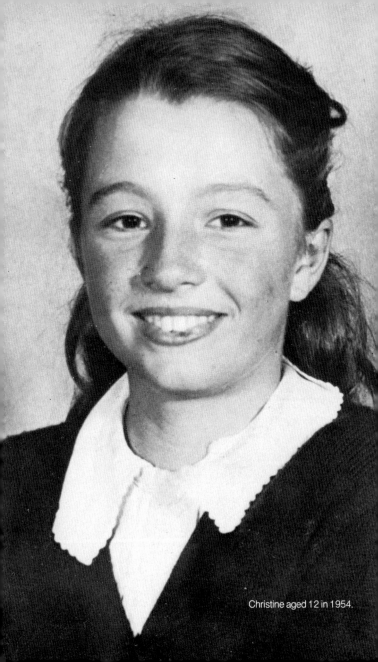
Christine aged 12 in 1954.

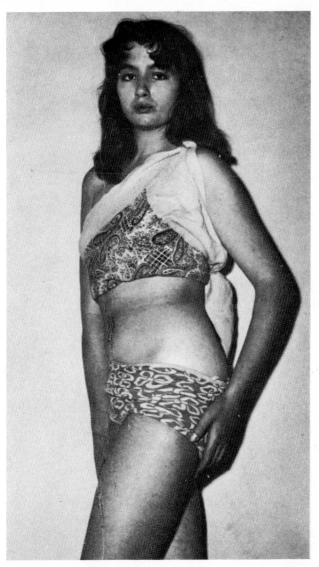

An early attempt at glamour in 1957.

At Murrays Cabaret Club
soon after arriving in London.

KENNETH H. BANDY LTD.

Mandy Rice-Davies in classic 50s modelling pose.

Where it all started. By the pool at Cliveden in 1961.

Leaving Stephen Ward's flat

Christine and Laura Knight snapped by the *Sunday Express* in 1963.

was going to call the police immediately. His friend was shouting too, he certainly didn't want a confrontation with the law, and finally I managed to get to the door, unlocked it, and Stephen's full weight fell in. He was livid, furious, and started shouting violently, something rare for him.

'How dare you behave like this in my house. Come on out at once. We are going to sort this out once and forever. Christine, make some coffee.'

I did as I was told as usual and when I brought it in to the sitting room there was another order for me.

'Now tell him in front of me.' I knew what he meant.

'I don't ever want to see you again, Lucky. I have told you before I have another boyfriend and that is my reason.' I felt very calm and safe standing beside Stephen. It made no difference to Lucky. It took both of them to drag him off and force him down the stairs. He was screaming all the way, begging them to let him whisper to me, he promised not to touch me. The two of them held him while I leaned forward to hear what he had to say.

'You've got to see me again, you must.'

'Yes, yes, I will.' Anything to pacify him and get those wild eyes out of my sight. I was shattered.

Stephen was shaken too and immediately phoned the police, informing them that a crazy drug addict had locked me up some weeks ago and had just attempted to do the same thing again at his house.

The police came round immediately. After all Dr Ward was a well-known personality with very high connections and Wimpole Mews was a very respectable area. I was examined for bruises and then Stephen sent me into the other room. Their conversation went on for quite a long time and when I was recalled the policeman gave me a very old-fashioned look.

'We won't be prosecuting, miss, because there aren't any marks on you, but if I were you I would go and see a doctor just to check you haven't caught anything unpleasant.' And that was all he said.

It was a long time before I realised that Stephen had passed the blame for any dope connections on to me. As ever, Stephen had used the situation to his own advantage and had wrung a virtual promise from the policeman that he would be allowed a visit to the Black Museum a ghoulish place where records and photographs of famous, violent murders were stored for police studies only; the public were not allowed in. His eyes were sparkling as he told me about it.

'Just think, little baby, they have pictures of Jack the Ripper's victims and all the weapons, whips, axes, knives and things that people have used against each other.'

My tribulations were banished from his mind at the prospect, and I, compliant as ever, went along with his latest enthusiasm.

CHAPTER FOUR

IF IT had rained on the weekend of 8 July, 1961, many lives
would have been different, including mine. If it had rained I
probably wouldn't have bothered to join Stephen at the
cottage at Cliveden because somehow or other I usually
ended up being the kitchen maid, peeling the potatoes and
washing the vegetables while he played chef. I would
probably have stayed in town and perhaps taken a
boyfriend back to the flat, something I only ever did when
Stephen was away.

But it didn't rain, and all week the newspapers had
carried variations on the 'Phew, What a Scorcher' theme.
London was sweltering and I was delighted to obey
Stephen's instructions to pick up some girl for him and get
some country air. A friend of mine, Leo, was going to drive
me down and first we did a desultory tour of the clubs to
have a looksee, but they were too stuffy to stay in and we set
off without a 'present' for Stephen. On the way we saw a
girl standing at a bus stop near the airport and offered her a
lift. Then we suggested she might like to come to a party at
Cliveden. It was that sort of weather, everyone in the world
felt free and glorious, and we were all in a happy mood
when we arrived.

Bill Astor was a generous man, allowing us the use of the
pool in the evenings when his stately guests had gone
indoors for dinner. He was also a considerate man in that he
kept a selection of swimsuits and trunks for those guests

who had come unprepared, so impromptu parties were not an infringement. Feeling happy and relaxed after a few drinks we voted for a swim and trooped up to the pool. It was a beautiful evening, almost dark by the time we got there, and I picked up any old bathers and plunged straight in. Water was my element and had been ever since I had learned to swim in the Wraysbury quarry pits. Stephen did not join in; he hated water, and wouldn't even take a bath because he considered water bad for the skin. So I swam across to where he was standing at the edge of the pool just to splash water on him. My costume wasn't very comfortable and as I hitched the straps up Stephen dared me to take it off. On a night like that, why not? It felt wonderful, I was a mermaid diving and rolling in the water, in my element.

We were shouting and laughing and splashing, making the kind of noises that carry in the clear evening air, and Stephen was the first to know that our games had attracted the attention of Bill Astor and his guests. Wicked as ever he grabbed my swimsuit from the edge of the pool, and chucked it behind a nearby bush.

'Now you're for it, little baby,' he chuckled.

'You brute,' I screamed. 'Give it back!'

By now I could see two figures in full evening dress approaching and there was I, stark naked. I made for the deep end where I had spotted a forgotten towel, clutched at it before Stephen could get to it, wrapped it round me as adequately as I could and then swam back to the shallow end to make as dignified a departure from the pool as possible. Scant is about the only word you can use to describe that towel.

I recognised Bill Astor, of course, and didn't mind joining in the laughter at my predicament until he and his companion (they had both obviously enjoyed a good dinner) thought it would be fun to give chase. Now I was a very nimble nineteen and able to keep well in front of them, but I was also desperately seeking my abandoned swimsuit while Stephen was doubled up with laughter. Bill decided to help me out by switching on the floodlights and at that moment Bill's other guests arrived.

For all Noel Coward later referred to me in his diaries as 'that little tart' he could not have staged the scene better. Imagine a dripping wet water sprite, hair streaming, tugging a skimpy wet towel to cover her private parts, two rather sheepish-looking, middle-aged gentlemen, slightly out of breath, and a collection of ladies in long evening dresses and tiaras accompanied by more gentlemen in formal evening clothes. It was not the best moment to be the centre of attention, but it was rescued by traditional English good manners. We were all introduced by Bill and that was how I met Jack Profumo, his companion who had chased me round the pool, and the Minister for War for Britain at the time.

We chatted for a while, Stephen making it clear that I was 'his little baby' which put everyone at ease and Bill asked us all up to the house for a drink. We were all in high spirits, the whole party. The very point of Cliveden weekends was for high-powered people to meet, talk, and relax. My little performance round the pool had helped everyone.

To me it was just another fun day. I had no idea that Jack Profumo had just had a heavy week with the Kuwait problem. I knew he was attracted to me but my training as a hostess at Murrays had taught me to recognise when a man needs to wind down and I didn't take his half-drunken jollity at all seriously. His wife, Valerie Hobson, was there so it was just all silly games. In retrospect it must have been galling for her watching her husband making a play for a chit of a girl and I, in my turn, must have been flattered by his attention. Thinking back, it probably had more to do with the fact that I was pulling the husband of a famous film star than his position in the government.

We were all a bit drunk and some time during the evening Jack offered to give me a conducted tour of Cliveden. It started out very elegantly with him showing me the huge paintings and telling me the dates of antique furniture. I was very impressed but could not imagine how anyone could want to live in so many rooms; what could you do in them? They were all dark and not in the least bit cosy. In the end I was rushing ahead to each door declaring that there couldn't be another one, this must be the last.

Jack was definitely in a chasing mood that night and the further we got away from the others the more he started cornering me, dodging round huge desks and tables. It was only for a kiss and a little surreptitious grope and really a million middle-aged men have done it before when they've had a few. On the way back to the drawing room we passed some suits of armour and I thought it would be a lark to try one on. It was and as I clanked my way down the corridor and back into the company there was an uproar of laughter.

The evening ended fairly early as Leo and I were driving back to London and just before we left Bill asked us all to come to his pool party the following day, Sunday. The reason I had to go back was quite ridiculous. Stephen had double dated; he had asked two girls each of whom were quite keen on him so at the last minute he had invited Eugene to the cottage for the day to share the load, so to speak. My role was to soothe their ruffled feathers and direct the way.

It was another splendid day and when we arrived at the pool the party was in full swing. Some were people from the night before like Ayub Khan, the President of Pakistan, Lord and Lady Dalkeith, and the Profumos; others had just dropped in. Introductions were made all round and if anybody thought it strange for the Russian Naval Attaché to meet the British War Minister in their bathing trunks nobody made any comment and it didn't interfere with anyone's enjoyment of the day. Stephen said later that he had had a secret moment savouring the irony but it was lost on most of us.

It was all frolics and fun with Bill, Eugene, Jack and the Pakistan President having a race from one end of the pool to the other swimming without moving their legs. They started at the deep end and when they came to the shallow end the winner, Jack, had both his feet at the bottom of the pool. Even Eugene laughed when Jack said, 'That'll teach you to trust the British.' Politics seemed light years away.

Then it was the girls' turn. Each of us clambered on to a man's shoulders – I was on Jack's – and the winner was the one who stayed afloat longest. I don't remember any of us taking the contest all that seriously, there seemed to be a lot of falling off and trying to get back on. I think we spent more time under the water than making headway.

It was really the first time I had seen Eugene relaxed. When he came to the flat to see Stephen he was always charming but distant. I think he was fascinated in a way because he couldn't make me out. For one thing I did very little but paint my face and have a good time, not a worthy citizen at all, but today he treated me like a woman, not just a unit in Stephen's life. Once or twice I caught sight of Stephen's wicked, twinkly grin as he noted Jack and Ivanov vying for my attention: Ivanov certainly saw Jack's hand accidentally brush against my calf. It was all very pleasant.

Even so, when Jack Profumo surreptitiously asked me for my telephone number I backed off. I didn't want to get involved.

'I live with Stephen,' I told him quickly. 'You'll have to ask him.' It was a neat bit of buck-passing and I thought that would be the end of that.

Eugene was driving me back to London as he had to report back to the Embassy. All the way back he talked about Russia, praising every aspect of it as if to cleanse his soul from the contamination of his day spent amongst the capitalists of Cliveden. A fast sports car overtook us, swerving dangerously in front of us and he cursed it roundly.

'In Russia,' (he began every sentence this way), 'in Russia you are simply stopped when you break the law and a mark is put in your driving book. Once you have three such marks you automatically cease to drive. Much better system, eh?'

I made a noncommittal sound. You didn't argue with Eugene and besides that he was looking devastatingly handsome, all tanned from his day in the sun and this was the first time we had been alone together.

'Do you have houses like Cliveden in Russia?'

'Yes, but they are for all the people to enjoy, not just a privileged few like today.' And he was off again on the glories of the Soviet Republic. I forbore to mention that for one so devoted to a system of equality he seemed remarkably keen to accompany Stephen around the smart cocktail circuit and live the high life in London. Whether Stephen had ever invited him to see the low life in Paddington I didn't know, but he certainly hadn't explored that area with us. But I was used to keeping my mouth shut in the presence of men and he rambled on all the way to Wimpole Mews. I invited him in for a cup of coffee but he had a better idea, he had a bottle of vodka in the boot of the car.

'In Russia,' he beamed, 'we drink vodka.'

In London we drank vodka with a vengeance too and it gave us both Mother Courage. He gave me the kiss we had both been waiting for and we made marvellous, passionate love. He was gorgeous, so utterly masculine, we were for a while totally swept away. And then it was over; he became instantly morose, as if ashamed at this excursion into

66

Western decadence, he had betrayed his wife and his country by wanting me. It was sad to see because he had made me feel wonderful, as far as I could see it was the perfect ending to a perfect day.

Stephen arrived home the following morning in a state of great excitement.

'Guess what, little baby? Jack Profumo wanted your telephone number so I gave it to him.' I shrugged, I wasn't particularly interested, I was still in a bit of a dreamy state from the night before, and Jack was just a married man who had made a playful pass at me, no more, and I had had plenty of experience of such men. 'But Christine, darling, don't you realise he is a very important man. He is the Secretary of State for War and he wants to see you again.' Stephen stopped suddenly and looked at me shrewdly. After all these years I was the proverbial open book to him. He grinned wickedly and knowingly. 'And what did you get up to last night with Eugene?'

'We talked,' I said defensively, trying to avoid Stephen's eye, then capitulating. 'Oh, Stephen, he was marvellous but he was so sad afterwards, I wish we hadn't.'

'Well, well, my naughty little baby, look at you, Eugene on one hand and Jack on the other, you'll be ruling the world next or starting the next war.'

Stephen's eyes were gleaming with devilish plans. He had already been contacted by MI5 the month before, on June 8, when he had been questioned about his close friendship with the Russian Naval Attaché. Stephen had explained that he had been introduced to Ivanov by Sir Colin Coote, editor of the *Daily Telegraph*, at a lunch at the Garrick. Sir Colin had been a patient of Stephen's and had commissioned him to do sketches at the Eichmann trials. They were old friends. Both Stephen and I had been very disappointed at the appearance of our 'cloak and dagger man'. Instead of a dashing James Bond or John Steed character, there was this tiny little man, not an inch over four foot eleven, in a bowler hat, steel-rimmed glasses and mackintosh. A rolled umbrella and briefcase completed his disguise. We had hooted with laughter when he had gone, having earnestly asked Stephen about the bridge parties at his club, the Connaught in Edgware Road, and whether Eugene had ever asked him for introductions to important persons or for any information of any kind.

Stephen had promised solemnly to get in touch if Eugene made any suspicious overtures. The little man eyed him passively, nodded, and left.

We should have been laughing on the other side of our faces for they had the last one, eventually.

Secretly the meeting must have stimulated Stephen's already lively imagination. He probably thought he was infinitely more suited to the job of undercover agent than the dreary little man who had visited him.

He built a picture of John Profumo for me that was both romantic and powerful: how he was really a Sicilian baron, how he had been the youngest Member of the House when he entered Parliament, how he had won an O.B.E. during the war, how he could even be a future Prime Minister. I was by now very intrigued to find out what Jack Profumo was really like, and when he telephoned me the following day to ask me out for a drive, I accepted immediately. As he arrived Stephen was on his way out to meet Eugene; they waved briefly to each other and I climbed into his big, black, shiny car. It was the most luxurious and comfortable car I had ever been in – I felt like a princess. He ordered the chauffeur to take us round London, past 10 Downing Street, which I had never seen before, and the barracks he was in charge of, where the War Ministry was housed. His commentary was relaxed and amusing, and I think he enjoyed impressing me. It was all very proper, and there was no back seat lunging, though he made his attraction to me very clear and after an hour or so he dropped me off at my front door.

'Shall I see you again?' he asked. I nodded agreement.

'I'll ring you tomorrow then. There is one thing . . . ' He sought for the right words. 'If you don't mind I'd rather not run into Stephen.'

I took it for granted that he had got hold of the wrong end of the stick about my relationship with Stephen. I was used to explaining to men that Stephen was not my lover, that we merely lived together, that he was a friend.

'Yes, I understand that,' he said, 'but I would rather see you elsewhere if he's at home. It will be better that way.'

'OK, ring me first, Stephen is at his surgery most afternoons anyway.'

I couldn't imagine what all the fuss was about. Stephen would know all about it anyway, we told each other everything. Sure enough Stephen was at home when I got in, waiting to hear all. I felt a bit as if I was letting him down when I reported we had only gone out for a drive seeing the sights, it was all too respectable for him.

'Is that all, Christine? Are you sure? Didn't he even make a pass at you?'

'Look, Stephen, if you think we had it off in the back of a government car while sailing past Downing Street all I can say is you have a very nasty mind.' I was laughing and trying to be severe at the same time. 'Anyhow he is going to phone me later this week.'

Stephen's excitement and interest did seem a bit over-charged for such a non-happening but I thought no more of it at the time. I didn't know that Stephen had already been in contact with the Security Services to inform them of the meeting between Ivanov and Profumo at the Astors' house at the weekend and that Eugene had shown a lot of interest in why the President of Pakistan had been there. Whether Eugene had asked Profumo directly, or had asked Stephen

69

to find out about the delivery of atomic secrets to West Germany by the Americans on that date, remains as classified information on their files. It only seemed to me that Stephen was, once again, getting his kicks out of my sex life and I was used to that by now. To me Jack was just a man and a nice one. Of course I was flattered; my head was turned. Jack telephoned a couple of days later to suggest another drive. This time he turned up in a Mini, borrowed for the occasion from a colleague, John Hare, and drove me to his house in Regents Park for a drink. It was a curious situation. I was nineteen, yet knowledgeable enough to know what was expected of me. But I was also a nineteen-year-old girl who had grown up in a sort of glorified caravan who now found herself conducted round a beautiful house where the owner would say nonchalantly of the dining room 'We often have the Queen here for dinner'. I stared at it fascinated, trying to imagine the scene, much as people do when they are conducted round historic houses.

Either side of the staircase were two very large china dogs. 'My wife bought me those,' he explained, as though that excused our ascent of the stairs. He showed me his office which held a huge desk and lots of telephones. One looked very odd and I asked about it.

'That's the scrambler. If I want to phone the Prime Minister direct I can use that and nobody can understand what is being said except the person on the other end.'

It's a pity he didn't pick it up and call 'Help' right there and then.

The next room was the bedroom, their bedroom, and that was where we made love for the first time. He was a strong, forceful lover, the kind of man who knows what he wants. Girls like me don't say 'no' when we meet them. It wasn't that he was particularly handsome but he had the allure of power – it would be the equivalent of fucking Marlon Brando for some women. Jack Profumo really impressed me. Unlike Eugene, who descended into the Slavic glooms afterwards, Jack was always nice, leisurely, there was never the feeling that having had his way all he wanted was to get the hell out.

It was a very, very well-mannered screw of convenience; only in other people's minds, much later, was it An Affair.

We continued to see each other, whenever Jack could get away from the War Office, at Wimpole Mews. He would ring saying that he would be round in an hour or so, first checking to see that the coast would be clear of Stephen, then drive himself round. The chauffeur-driven car never appeared again, all was discretion. And now here all cynics can join hands for the bitter laugh that was to come: the idea that Jack's association with me was ever a threat to security.

Jack Profumo came round for a straightforward screw, no more, no less. As he came through the door he had only one thing in mind . . . and that was to get me into bed. His hands were all over me all the time and it was very pleasant but it was not the stuff of which Mata Haris are made. Over a cigarette and a coffee afterwards the conversation was desultory, polite. He would tell me that he had been away to Germany or Wolverhampton for some boring Army function and sometimes he would make me laugh by explaining that when he gave the salute he would separate his index and third finger in a private 'up yours' gesture, but that was the nearest we ever got to sedition. Mostly, he would turn the conversation to my background, not my London one but my, to him, totally strange upbringing. Real poverty was something he had never known and he was fascinated by my stories about my mum and dad, all of us living together in a converted railway carriage.

When he first heard that I was an only child he took it for granted that I must have been spoiled, that had to be the way with only daughters. He cannot have been naive, he

71

had been a pleasure-seeking bachelor until the age of thirty-nine, but he never queried my present way of life. He often offered me money but for some reason I could not accept it from him, he was somehow too grand. I would have felt debased in a way I did not accepting money from businessmen. Perhaps I thought he was special, a privilege. Instead he bought me presents, scent from Fortnums, a lighter from Aspreys, and I cherished them. As we got to know each other better – perhaps acquainted would be a more accurate word – I accepted twenty pounds from him to buy my mother a treat. Another nail in our coffins. As I said, at the time I had no qualms about accepting money from other men and one day, just as Jack was leaving, Jim Eylan arrived at the door for his usual visit. Jim obviously recognised him but behaved in true Army fashion; no names, no pack drill.

The same could not be said of Stephen, who was having a field day around town. Curiously he was careful not to mention to the Security Services that I had bedded both the War Minister and a Russian Naval Attaché within a few days of each other, but the information was assiduously leaked to his eager cronies in London as a juicy bit of gossip. Like all good stories it improved with the telling and before long it was well known that as Eugene left by the back door, Jack was panting up the front stairs. The sad truth was that Eugene was genuinely remorseful about his lapse of morals and his very occasional calls at the house at that time were only to pick Stephen up and drive him elsewhere. He did not want to bump into me at all. It is galling to have to say so, but my activities, in or out of bed, were of no interest to MI5 at the time. The only person arousing anxiety in them was Dr Stephen Ward, who had both Eugene Ivanov and John Profumo calling at his house. What to Stephen was an escapade, an opportunity to stand at parties and say 'But, my dear, you do not know the half. . . . ' and thus ensure he was the centre of attention was to them a possibly dangerous liaison.

They began to investigate Stephen and wonder at his motives for introducing Eugene into Londons' exclusive inner society. They were convinced there was more to the friendship than a mutual love of bridge. It would have been incomprehensible to them that Stephen just liked throwing a spanner in the works, that to be first with a titillating story was of prime importance in his life. They were looking for something evil, and Stephen, irresponsible, fantasising, self-important Stephen, was about to give it to them.

We were at home exchanging all our news, who we had seen, what we had done – he knew every detail of my affair with Jack, though I didn't know he kept notes of the days and the times. We were in bed, cuddling, propped up against the pillows watching the television.

'Why don't you ask Jack about the bomb, Christine?'

'What bomb, Stephen?' I asked innocently. I never read the papers except sometimes for the showbiz parts.

'You know, when the Americans are going to deliver their atomic secrets to West Germany.'

'Don't be silly, Jack wouldn't tell me a thing like that, and in any case I wouldn't dream of asking him.' I was a bit put out, I was sure Stephen only wanted to know so as to add to his status of being on the 'inside'. He was already beginning to exaggerate his contacts with the security people.

'I was only joking, little baby, I just thought it would be amusing if you knew.' He kissed me goodnight and went off to sleep chuckling to himself, no doubt thinking of the Secretary of State for War giving me one in his bed.

My affair with Jack Profumo was probably doomed to be short-lived by its very nature but it was certainly shortened by Stephen's meddling. About a month after our first meeting Jack was taken on one side by Sir Norman Brook who was Secretary to the Cabinet and warned off too close an association with a Dr Stephen Ward, as the man apparently had close connections with the Assistant Russian Naval Attaché and MI5 were not entirely sure he was the diplomat he made out to be. My name was not mentioned, which must have been an almighty relief to Jack. Jack recognised the need for caution and sent me a little note to break our next date. I popped it in the drawer where I kept all my letters and thought no more about it.

One evening Jack proposed setting me up in a flat of my own. I couldn't think why, I was happy living with Stephen and had had enough of being owned when I lived with Peter Rachman. I turned the offer down, giving him only the reason that I was happy as I was.

'But darling, I won't be able to go on seeing you while you live here with Stephen.' We were outside my front door now. I turned to him.

'Now this is silly, you know I don't have sex with Stephen. It's nothing like that. I don't know why you hate Stephen so.'

Jack didn't answer. He seemed to me to be sulking.

'Well, I can't see you again if you remain here,' he said finally.

'All right then, don't see me again,' I cried, and flounced off, slamming the front door behind me. To me the choice was simple; between a clandestine affair where we couldn't even go to a restaurant together for fear of scandal, and living with a good, true friend who made me laugh. Upstairs I shed a few tears of rage and frustration over what I thought was Jack's pig-headed possessiveness and decided to say nothing to Stephen because I thought he would have insisted that I mustn't let him stand in my way.

Looking back, I think it is a pity I didn't tell Stephen. He was a foolish, mischievous man but he would have been shrewd enough, knowing Jack's obsession with me, to realise that the powers-that-be were watching. He might even have realised that we were both in greater danger than we knew. I had one more note from Jack saying that if I wanted to see him again I could get in touch with him but I didn't bother to read the letter twice and never saw him again. The 'Great Affair' was over, and, I assumed, forgotten.

But I had bargained without the nosiness of the press. If MI5 were unaware of my existence, newspaper reporters were not. It doesn't take long for juicy stories of that nature to get from the cocktail circuit to Fleet Street. Too many impoverished young men from impeccable backgrounds supplement their incomes by selling information to the gossip columns. In their case it wasn't the security angle that interested them but the sexual one. Nor was it adultery in high places – there was always plenty of that going on – but once again the connection with Stephen Ward. If MI5 were worried about Profumo associating with Stephen because of Ivanov, Fleet Street were enthralled at the prospect of Profumo being possibly connected with Ward and his orgies. They too began to investigate Ward more thoroughly.

In Dr Stephen Ward were gathered all the potential ingredients for a great sexual scandal that could encompass household names like Sir Winston Churchill, who was a patient, the Royal Family whom he had drawn, and an endless supply of pretty girls, mostly from ordinary backgrounds, whom he had cultivated and possibly corrupted by introducing them to a decadent High Society where whips and chains were handed round with the After Eights. Add to that a Cabinet Minister, the man responsible for the safety of our Sovereign Queen, and what more could you want? They were prepared to bide their time.

Meanwhile at the little flat in Wimpole Mews the usual

stream of visitors would be dropping in for a cup of coffee, to talk about the Berlin Crisis, to sit for Stephen. Bill Astor still called, though Profumo's name was never mentioned. Eugene stayed longer; the conversations were more political and still way above my head despite my first-hand experience of the corridors of power, but Stephen's interest in the behind-the-scenes mechanics of political life grew, and with it his self-importance. He would try to tell me the stories behind the headlines, that a ship that had sunk held top secret equipment, snippets of information that excited him. Stephen was still going to sex parties, usually at Mariella Novotny's. These parties were always very exclusive, but Stephen was particularly thrilled with the latest at Novotny's – a man who got his kicks by serving dinner wearing nothing but a mask. He was rumoured to be a Cabinet Minister and Stephen assured me that the man was Ernie Marples, but then he mentioned so many names. One day I asked him idly if he thought Eugene was a spy, I don't know why.

'So what if he is, little baby, there's a lot of money in spying.'

Afterwards it turned out that Stephen often cashed cheques from Eugene at his club; the sums were too small to be mistaken for pay-offs but they could have been to defray his expenses. Stephen was notoriously reluctant to put his hand in his pocket.

And all the time Mandy and I would sneak off for the occasional afternoon or evening out together. Our meetings had to be secret, because Peter thought I was a bad influence on her and Stephen thought likewise of her influence on me. He regarded her as mercenary and vulgar and the fact that he had screwed her once did not alter his opinion. They were both right, of course, our need to be with people our own age often led us into trouble, though Mandy was mostly faithful to Peter while she lived with him because she appreciated all that he did for her. He showered her with gifts of furs, a car, jewellery and money and in return she gave him sex and a sort of happiness. He was the first man she had ever had a long relationship with and I think he loved her to the best of his ability, which, after his awful life, wasn't a great deal but it was all he had to give.

Certainly when he found us enjoying ourselves down in Bournemouth (he had taken her there for the tennis, one of his passions, and had had to return to London urgently so I had joined her for a larky few days) it was me he walloped and her whom he forgave, a rare occurrence for him.

It was to Mandy I confided my interest in Jack Profumo and she was pleased for me, hoping – such was Peter's influence on her – that it meant that both my dealings with the West Indian community and Stephen's hold on my life were coming to an end.

CHAPTER FIVE

MANDY'S HOPES for me were about to be dashed; Stephen was restless again and so was I. We were ready for a bit of fun again.

Alfred Marks and his wife, who were great friends of Stephen's, had dropped by for a drink, sensibly bringing it with them as they knew full well Stephen kept none in the house. Stephen was regaling them with my adventures as well as bringing them up to date with the rest of London's bad habits, telling them the shocking story of my abduction by a black man who had also come round to the house and attacked us both. He was a great raconteur and managed to turn the whole thing into an exhilarating and amusing tale, ignoring the fact that even though we had not been troubled with Lucky's presence since the night he had called the police, we were still plagued with phone calls from him in the middle of the night.

Thoroughly wound up by his own enthusiasm, Stephen turned to me. 'Come on, little baby, let's go down to the jungle and hear the drums beat again, you only live once, it might as well be dangerously.'

Alfred and his wife didn't take much persuading. If it was only half as strong as Stephen had described it, it was well worth a visit and any qualms I may have had were offset by the assembled company. Lucky was there all right at the restaurant, but Stephen made such a song and dance about him, pointing him out and making loud jokes, that he didn't

78

stir from his seat. I was very nervous, which added to Stephen's thrills, but the evening passed off without event.

It had been a stupid, provocative gesture, another of Stephen's empty ways of showing off, and I was soon being haunted by Lucky again. He began furtively hanging round the streets near our house so that I never knew when I was going to catch a glimpse of him in a shop window or if I would see him crossing the road ahead of me. It was a nightmare driving me mad, and I felt hemmed in on all sides. Also I was tiring of Stephen's company. I wanted to be with friends of my own age.

I took a flat in Dolphin Square, slap bang in the middle of the Chelsea rave-up set and it suited me fine. Mandy, having had one of her regular tiffs with Peter, had moved in for a while, but I was running wild; she couldn't stand the pace and was grateful to go back to the safety of Peter. But I had a new bunch of friends; an ex-racing driver called Paul, and a girl called Linda and her black boyfriend.

By now I was into pot-smoking and life was a continuous party. There was Stephen dropping in, and a lot of very odd people who felt free to call at any time, bringing with them more friends, bottles or smokes; people could do what they liked, and did. If we weren't at home we were creating havoc round the pubs and clubs. It was wonderful to be free, young and daring. We were all so far out of it that we thought nothing of wandering around or answering the door entirely in the nude.

Through a girlfriend of mine I met a barrister who was a masochist and I used to whip him and make him grovel at my feet. The more I insisted on his being punished for such disgraceful behaviour the more excited he became. He never wanted sex with me and when he had come he would have a quick wash, get dressed, thank me formally and pay. I suppose I didn't find it strange after Stephen and I quite enjoyed it. It was all in his mind and I doubt if he would have recognised me in the street. It all had to be acted out very seriously, one snigger or giggle from me and that would have been the end of a very lucrative relationship. He probably went back to work then to send some poor sod to jail but I didn't worry about such things in those days.

I was working as a model, too, not exactly making the front cover of *Vogue* yet, but earning a living of sorts. In any case there was plenty of money around, most of it from the male hustlers who were busy screwing heiresses. I was having fun and had escaped Lucky Gordon's clutches. Or so I thought.

I was out having a drink in a pub in Chelsea with Paul who, though he stayed at the flat at weekends, was not a lover, when Lucky walked in. Somebody, probably Stephen, had told him where I was hanging out these days. Although everyone knew about Lucky and his violence, blacks, like pot, were part of the newly-liberated, fashionable scene. I had gained cachet through Stephen's stories of our adventures in downtown Paddington; the nearest that lot had ever got to meeting a black man was shaking hands with a visiting jazz musician and telling him how they collected his records at public school. So Paul insisted that it was time for bygones to be bygones and invited Lucky back to the flat for a drink; our own private, token black. Since we were already out of our minds we didn't notice that Lucky was too. We had also not noticed that in the letter-cage on the back of the front door was an axe, left by the previous tenant. Whatever Lucky's intentions when he came to the party his brain did a flip as the door closed and he spotted it. Within seconds he was rampaging round the room, swinging it at anyone in sight, and let me tell you they weren't in sight for long. Quicker than Flynn they bolted.

Only Linda had the guts to stay and for two days he terrorised both of us. It sounds (and seems) unbelievable now that any man could screw, sleep, demand food and cups of tea incessantly without either of us being able to escape. But it is the truth and ever since, when I have read accounts of terrorists or kidnappers having held people for weeks, I have known how they felt. Any humiliation is better than death. Any move of mine that wasn't totally acquiescent was rewarded with slaps and punches though he never once touched Linda. Her loyalty, fear for my life, was immense, matched only by her amazement at the games I played to calm him down. When the phone rang I had to pretend to the friends at the other end that I was fine, just a bit tired, not that there was a lunatic with an axe standing over me. They were not unduly worried, they were living their lives elsewhere.

Finally we ran out of cigarettes and food, and by that time I had convinced Lucky that I was once again his devoted slave. I displayed the empty cupboard.

'Someone will have to run down to the shop on the corner,' I told him.

'Send her.' He pointed at an all-too-willing Linda.

'No, no, my dear, she will only call the police.' He saw the sense in this and agreed to go himself so long as I gave him the keys.

The problem was solved before he reached the stairs. Linda and I slipped the safety catch and rang the police. They were round in seconds and caught him on the stairs. This time I had evidence of grievous bodily harm – my face was covered in great red welts. They took Lucky and charged him while I was left wondering how long he would get and how to keep it out of the papers so mum wouldn't find out. I was still worrying when the phone rang. It was his brother begging me to drop the charges, telling me of the long line of convictions Lucky already had and that this time he would be going down for a long stretch, that he wouldn't stand a chance inside on account of being coloured. They promised to make sure I never saw Lucky again.

Like a fool I listened to him. I didn't particularly want to put anyone inside – I am not a vengeful person – but outweighing any such moral niceties was the spectre of all the sordid details being relayed to strangers in court and my mum's reaction if she found out I had been involved with a coloured person.

I rang the police to drop the charges but they insisted on coming to see me again.

'You must understand, Miss Keeler, that he is a very dangerous man. He has a string of convictions behind him, one for the attempted murder of a girl. You were fortunate this time, next time you may not be.'

I was adamant and they were furious with me but they could do nothing.

They had been right, of course, and the next day Lucky was back in Dolphin Square, lurking round corners, leaning against the wall outside. The police could only remove him from the premises and as soon as they released him he would return. They considered us both a bloody nuisance.

It was time to run back to Stephen again; another fling at independence was over. Once more it was lovely to be home but things had changed while I was away. Stephen had grown wilder in his chase after erotic pleasure; he was really into prostitutes now, and some of them looked very strange indeed, battered and depraved. When he brought them back the door to his bedroom was always firmly shut – I was no longer needed as a participant.

And still I was pursued by Lucky. The nightmare level of my life grew to a state of daylight dread. I was afraid to answer the phone, to go out alone, even to be alone at home. Sometimes he would leave me alone for a week and during that time the suspense was more unbearable than the attacks I was imagining. Slowly his obsession became mine. My nerves were stretched beyond endurance. I do not know why I did what I did next – whether the fear and violence had become a fixation in my mind, or whether I felt drawn towards a fatalistic self-destruction. I think I would have done anything to get it over. One day I woke up feeling very calm, knowing there was only one way to find peace, to rid myself of this extraordinary and almost eerie state of affairs.

I went alone to the club where I knew I would find him, utterly indifferent to any danger I might be facing. I had to resolve the situation. I felt a moment of fear (or was it excitement? The two are very close) when I saw him. He crossed the room quickly, grabbed my arm and ordered coffee.

'I have to talk to you, Lucky, I cannot allow you to go on making my life such a misery.' I tried to explain to him gently that he had nothing to gain by frightening me all the time.

He gripped my arm tightly but for once there was no violence between us. 'Look, Christine, you don't understand, I'm in love with you. I don't mean any harm to you but I just can't go away. Even to see you on the other side of the street is better than not seeing you at all, to hear your voice on the phone is enough, I can't help myself. You don't give yourself a chance to love me because I am black, you are afraid all the time what people will think, you are afraid to love a black man. Have you never loved desperately?'

I thought of Manu and the terrible scenes I had made, of being overcome with longing for one person and the awful pain. I knew too that my rejection did come from him being black and from what other people would say. Stephen would turn away from me not for Lucky's colour but for his lack of polish. My mum, who couldn't tell the difference between a black bus conductor and an African ambassador, would be shocked, and I was deeply confused. I answered only his last question.

'Yes, Lucky, I have been in love.'

'Then you know how it feels.' He put his free hand over his heart and I nodded.

'So you promise that if I see you sometimes, it will only be occasionally because I am trying to build my career. You will never, ever, behave like you did last time?'

Lucky was delighted with the proposition, his face alight with relief and happiness. 'Let's get out of here, my brothers have a house far away from here, let's go and visit them for a day, maybe a few days?'

'But you do promise you will never attack me, frighten me again?'

He gave his solemn promise that now I had come to him he would never again harm a hair on my head.

Like most of the promises I have received from men in my life, both white and black, from lords and lawyers, it meant nothing, but I did not know that at the time. I thought that by facing my innermost fears, I had won.

Life throws up some strange contrasts for the adventurous, and whatever my faults I was that. The room I shared with Lucky at his brothers' house could not have been more different to the one in Regents Park with its brocade curtains and the direct line to the Prime Minister next door. It was barely furnished and his sister-in-law hung her washing there. There was a single bed, a chair, and a chest of drawers with a small television on top, but here I was treated like royalty, a princess. Gone was the snarling man with manic, darting eyes; in his place was a gentle, devoted man whose eyes were deep brown with kindness. The hands that had held a knife at my throat, an axe over my head, now fetched a flannel and basin to wash me tenderly, a brush to stroke my hair. He brought my meals to

84

me and fed me, slowly and amorously. We made love for days.

I suppose it was my first real experience of sex, how it could and should be, which must sound odd coming from a girl who had been around as much as I had, but it was the first time I had been properly loved. I had been used by many men, had allowed them to use me; sex was something they wanted and money was something I needed. The men who pay for sex are interested only in their own gratification – which does not mean to say they are all pigs and brutes, just that there is a difference between fancying a screw and making love. I am not saying this was the first time I had had an orgasm, because it wouldn't be true, but though most men desired me, Lucky, for those few days, made me feel beloved, a woman.

It couldn't last, of course. The longer I stayed the greater his dreams of our future together grew, but the nasty little realist at the back of my mind was recognising that the honeymoon was over. I had to get back to town, to Stephen. He was relieved to see me but none too pleased with my prolonged absence.

'And where the hell have you been? I've had your mother and everyone on the phone wondering where you are, I'm sick of making excuses.'

He berated me for my foolhardiness in going to the club alone but as I told him of Lucky waiting on me hand and foot, washing me all over and becoming my slave, he was totally beguiled. I had returned with a new naughty story and all was forgiven. Calculating little cow that I was, I had already planned my next move. I guessed that Lucky would be phoning Wimpole Mews before long and as the phone rang I told Stephen that I had already arranged to hide out at Michael Lambton's for a while.

Stephen threw his hands in the air in exasperation as I ran down the stairs to the waiting mini-cab. I was impossible,

85

and he was right; a gypsy, a wayward, rebellious child, but still his little baby, and I went with his blessing.

Michael was just as welcoming, he thought he was rescuing me from Stephen's clutches as by now Stephen's reputation as a wicked influence on all he met was well established round the gossip circuit.

Living with Michael was civilising and I enjoyed it. I began to forget my wantonness, the wild escapades, and to realise the value of an ordered life. Michael knew very little about me, his own view of life was sheltered, the people he mixed with may have thought they were rakes but they knew nothing of the Stephens and the Luckys of this world, and I wasn't about to tell him. I liked the way he was both firm and masculine without needing to be superior. He drank a lot, but we were happy, and he bought me a ruby and diamond engagement ring. I was contemplating settling down.

Then along came trouble. Mandy again. She wouldn't admit that she was tiring of Peter (Mandy could never tire of a constant supply of money) but her ambitions were sprouting again. She felt ready to try her luck in America and suggested it was time I did the same.

Mandy had been a busy little bee making connections in the film world. Nina Gadd, who had introduced us to the 21 Club the previous year, had become her best friend so I guessed that more connections had been made there than on the studio floor. Nevertheless I was willing to be swept along with their plans. America. Going to New York. Of course I wasn't going to be left behind, no sir.

Mandy talked grandly of some tentative commercial. Nina, who was staying with Stephen (he couldn't bear to come home to an empty house and she was paying him a fiver a week rent, something I had never done) would join us three weeks later. We were to leave in two weeks' time, all I needed was five hundred quid.

I rushed home to Michael who dampened my enthusiasm with a blank refusal, he had no intention of 'lending' me money, having learned his lesson in Comeragh Road. I sulked, I wheedled, I cajoled to no avail. Finally I declared that I would find it somehow and deliberately dressed myself to the nines, taking my time. I was not an expert for nothing. He gave in.

Cussed as ever, as soon as I had won I changed my mind. It seemed silly to go back to my old ways with Mandy when I was happy and secure with Michael. I rang Mandy to tell her I wasn't going, news which didn't please her one whit. Mandy does not like to have her plans thwarted; she rang back half an hour later to apologise for having 'accidentally' let slip my whereabouts to Lucky Gordon. She had stitched me up well and truly. She knew damn well I daren't let Michael become involved with any 'black' scandal, because it would ruin his name in his publishing business. I had no option but to give in.

Michael, taking note of my determination to go to the States, had been secretly negotiating a deal to spend six months out there himself. He, too, would be in New York in three weeks' time and we would set up home there. I was going to start life anew, and two very excited young girls set sail from Southampton on a hot day in July 1962. The events of the previous July had disappeared from my mind and neither one of us could have known, had we the slightest premonition, that the following July we would be standing in the witness box at the Old Bailey.

Our devotion to our respective lovers, Michael and Peter, was very short-lived. We had a rare old time on the boat, creating havoc among crew and passengers alike. It was all very glamorous and we were thoroughly spoiled. We arrived in New York confident that we were all they had been waiting for, and rushed round the clubs showing off our London Look (our skirts were just above the knee and quite shocking to the Paris-influenced Americans) and our London dancing which was sexy and suggestive. We were a rave.

It was another good thing that couldn't last. We had mistakenly heard that Fire Island was *the* place to go for the weekend. Well, it was if you were a fella. The whole place was totally gay, which wasn't exactly our scene but we were stuck there with our suitcases and our posh English accents. Rescue came in the form of two policemen who organised a hotel room for us after reassuring themselves that we were not a couple of dykes. As we were not allowed to take up residence till late in the afternoon we spent the day on the beach giggling at the gays; the parading and open flaunting of homosexuality was quite new to us, since back in London men were still being sent to jail for picking each other up. The age of consenting adults was not yet with us.

It was hot, far hotter than anywhere else I had ever been, and displaying true Brit foolishness, by the end of the day we were burnt to a cinder. The hotel doctor was called and by the time our two policemen arrived all we could do was beg them to smooth the soothing lotion on us. It must have been one of the most frustrating evenings of their lives.

It also ruined Mandy's chances for her commercial and consequently our survival money. Being broke in America is no fun – the great credit system does not extend to impecunious strangers and we could not risk a repeat of our South of France performance. Mandy was, as ever, quick to look after Number One. She was booked on a plane back to Peter almost before I had realised how desperate a situation I was in. There was no way I could survive three weeks in New York on my own without money – my fear of that was greater than my fear of flying and of cabling Michael (reversed charges of course) for my air fare.

He was not especially glad to see me return so soon and furious with Mandy for having cocked things up so much.

He was already jealous of any friends I made on my own (and I must admit they did always seem to cost him money) but I couldn't face the idea of being stuck in America with him, away from everyone I knew, so the inevitable happened. I went back to Stephen.

Just as inevitably Lucky Gordon heard I was back and the terrible rigmarole of the nuisance phone calls and hanging around began again. Stephen had recently bumped into an old friend, Paula Hamilton-Marshall, who lived in a flat round the corner in Devonshire Street with her younger brother, John, and Kim a girl from one of the clubs, turned photographer. Paula also had West Indian friends and Stephen and I would go round there for a coffee. It was at Paula's that I met Johnny Edgecombe and was immediately attracted to him; he seemed better educated and more intelligent than his compatriot Lucky, and it was natural to explain to him the trouble I was having.

'I just wish I could get hold of a gun,' I told them. 'I swear to God that it's not because I want to kill him, I just think that if he saw it in my hand it would frighten him enough to stay away from me.'

I may have been dramatising but like many such bold statements, this one came home to roost. Someone knew someone who knew where I could acquire a gun and arranged for me to go to a club to meet their contact. I paid a very respectable bloke £25 for a German gun and two magazines with seven bullets in. At the weekend I went to some woods near my parents' home and tried it out by firing a bullet into a tree. It worked, and I felt safe carrying it in my handbag. My altruistic ideals changed with the knowledge that I could make it work. If Lucky Gordon came at me again I was going to kill him. I would go to prison but he would be out of my life forever.

He proved his name right when he attacked me a few weeks later. I had moved out of Wimpole Mews again.

Stephen was changing fast, our mothering-fathering-babying relationship didn't seem to work any more. He was even more fascinated by weird prostitutes, and was drawing pornographic pictures more than portraits – very realistic, all big dicks and spunk, though only for his own pleasure. He kept them in his wardrobe but I never saw him flashing them around. Socially his life was pretty much the same, with the constant flow of friends dropping in. Ivanov was still a regular, but I found I wanted to be with people my own age. Kim, our photographer friend and I took a flat in Notting Hill Gate and Johnny Edgecombe became my lover. He was a marvellous lover but not a keen worker, he had no job. I had begun to break into modelling, I did a Camay television commercial for West Germany but we were still short of money. Mandy visited us when she got fed up with Peter and sometimes we would pop round to see Stephen. Life was casual and easy, and I didn't bother to carry my gun any more. We all thought Johnny had frightened Lucky away, as all our conversations were dominated by how to get Lucky off my back.

We were wrong. As I came out of a hairdresser's with an American girlfriend one day Lucky sprang at me, knocking me to the ground and screaming abuse. The noise must have sounded like a full scale riot. I was hollering, the American girl was hollering and people all round started yelling 'Get the police.' The struggle didn't last long before Lucky realised his danger and fled. I was all for sticking it out and taking proceedings but the American hadn't got a permit to stay and she would have been deported.

I grabbed a cab and hurtled home. Johnny then telephoned Lucky and inadvertently let him know where we were living. I knew what that would mean. Kim went to live on her own in Grosvenor Square, Johnny moved around the corner knowing that we still had Lucky to contend with, and insisted that we should bring this to a head and confront Lucky once and for all. Johnny calmed me down and I didn't notice how upset he was over my bruises. When he suggested that the sensible thing to do was to go to the club and confront Lucky with the fact that we were living together and that there was no room in my life for Lucky, I agreed.

As soon as Johnny and I arrived, Lucky, who was still in a mad rage, picked up a chair and aimed it at us. I was all for running for dear life but Johnny's temper flared instantly. There was Lucky chasing me, Johnny chasing him, girls screaming and the men in the room going ominously still. It was all over in a moment, Lucky was cornered, and Johnny's hand reached into his pocket for a knife. He slashed Lucky right down the side of his face, from his forehead to his chin. It was horrible, the blood spurted everywhere, streamed down his face and clothes. Lucky was screaming with anger and pain.

'I'll get you for this, you'll go inside. Somebody get the police.'

We had no time to spare. The club was The Allnighters in Wardour Street and the police were never very far away. Johnny knew, too, that Lucky's brothers would be seeking revenge. We ran to a telephone box and called a mini-cab, and while we waited for it I called Stephen who begged me to come home.

'I can't, Stephen, he will be worse when he gets out of hospital, we've got to go into hiding for a while. I'll ring you when it's safe.'

Looking back, it was a typically generous offer from Stephen. My sort of wretched troubles must have been the very last thing he needed on his doorstep. That night was Saturday, October 27, 1962 and all week long the world had been holding its breath over the Cuban crisis. The four-minute warning, which was all any of us were going to get if there was a full-scale nuclear war, had been practically the only subject of conversation all week. In true British fashion there had been a lot of sick jokes bandied about but to Stephen the subject had been both serious and important.

Stephen and Eugene Ivanov had been close friends for two years and during that time they had had many discussions and some disagreements about politics. Also during that time Stephen had introduced Eugene to many people in high places and, being Stephen, had doubtless mentioned their sexual peccadilloes. He must have been extraordinarily useful to the Russians, though his loyalties were to the British whom he was very eager to serve. I am sure Stephen Ward had no idea that he was just an amateur in a field full of very shrewd professionals when he offered himself up as an intermediary between the Russians and the government during that crisis week. I remember Mandy and I going round to Wimpole Mews that week and Stephen's excitement at being in the thick of things.

Eugene had suggested that Stephen use his contacts in high places to bring about a summit conference in London. Stephen rang Bill Astor and Sir Godfrey Nicholson for an introduction to the Foreign Office. Of course he couldn't think it out politically, any more than I could understand the manoeuvres, but he was a pacifist hoping to save the world from war and probably impressed by Ivanov's trust. His urgent activities were a terrible mistake, and those cold, professionals' eyes and ears kept watch and listened to his boastings as he hinted around town how close he had been to the government during their dark hour.

Needless to say, that night when I phoned him with my troubles I was totally unconcerned about world events, I had my own world of violence to contend with. And yet the two were to be curiously entwined within a few weeks.

While Johnny and I remained in hiding in Brentwood, where he had some German friends, I kept in touch with

Stephen. He told me that Lucky had been round with seventeen stitches in his hand.

'Give them to Christine,' he had said, 'she's going to be needing them.'

Stephen was laughing as he told me this but my blood ran cold. He was still extraordinary, the Cuban crisis had ended with the Russian ships turning back, much to Eugene's chauvinist fury (they had been at Cliveden with Lord Arran and Bill when the news came through and Eugene's lack of manners had shocked the English gents) but Stephen, who had been so passionately involved, merely moved on, looking for the next thrill. My drama with Johnny and Lucky provided one, and Mandy was busy with another.

Way back in the early autumn Stephen had asked me if I would mind if an Indian doctor used my room one afternoon a week for the pursuit of sex. The man had offered him £25 a week. It never occurred to me to say 'Why my room? Why not yours?' Stephen had also implied that if the man was looking for a screw I could earn some extra that way; the days of telling his little baby not to seek the easy way were long since gone.

I wasn't particularly affronted but I wasn't interested either, so when I left to move in with Johnny and his German friends, he passed the invitation on to Mandy. I don't really know the details of the deal because I was stuck out in Brentwood but Mandy moved into my room at Wimpole Mews to be available to Dr Emil Savundra. Knowing Mandy she was probably testing the waters because she left some of her things at Peter's, but she must have guessed that Savundra was even richer than Peter Rachman.

It was the end of November and I was fed up with Brentwood, so I rang Mandy for a chat and the news. I could hardly understand what she was saying, she was sobbing so hard. Peter Rachman was dead and she was distraught. Poor Mandy, he was the nearest thing to love she had ever known and now she was all alone. I told Johnny I had to be by her side and reluctantly he let me go. Once again as the wheels moved I felt the burden of being possessed by another slip from my shoulders. I can't stand being cooped up with anyone for long.

Mandy was in a terrible state and Stephen was not helpful. He couldn't, or wouldn't, take her grief seriously and, much as I felt sorry for her, it was difficult not to laugh as he told everyone that Mandy's first words when she heard of Peter's death were 'Did he make a will?' He had, but she wasn't in it. She wasn't even allowed into Bryanston Mews to collect her things.

I stayed with Paula for a few days till I found a flat in Great Cumberland Place, everyone was sworn to secrecy so that neither Lucky nor Johnny would know where to find me. I had had enough of my bad ways. I was sick of my own stupidity, I was tired of being hounded from one place to another. I was tired of violence, tired of scenes. I resolved to change and moved in with a nice girl called Rosemary who was a dress designer at Wallis. I wasn't going to screw for money ever again.

Unfortunately I wasn't tired of pot smoking.

With Rosemary's help – she being a good example of being serious about a career – I started going the rounds of the modelling jobs again. I landed one very quickly, a television commercial for Knight's Castile soap. Very pleased with myself I went round to Paula with the news and on the spur of the moment we decided to look in on Mandy to cheer her up with the fact that life wasn't over, and that there was still a big world out there for us all.

It bloody nearly wasn't for Mandy. She had taken an enormous overdose of sleeping pills and would have been dead by the morning. Stephen was out to dinner and in any case would not have bothered to look in on his return. We called an ambulance and she was pumped out. I hid the suicide note because to try and kill yourself was a criminal offence in those days. When she returned to Stephen's flat we all tried to help her but she was very depressed and defeated, not at all our bouncy Mandy.

December 14, 1962, was a Friday, I was due to make my commercial on the Monday following and I needed a few things. I decided to drag Mandy out on a shopping spree, thinking that if I got her out of the house she might begin to come to life again. She still didn't want to move from her bed, and was probably still hoping for rescue from beyond the grave. She begged me to ring Mrs Rachman to see if Peter had made any arrangement for her. I refused, I had already given in and told the family that she had attempted suicide and I knew her position was hopeless. It was time to get on with life.

Slowly, very slowly, she made a move. I knew that if I could just get her out of her slough of despond she would be fine. I didn't know how shallow that slough was going to prove to be. Then the telephone rang and I picked it up automatically. It was Johnny Edgecombe.

'Look, Johnny, I'm not living here, Mandy is now and you know how difficult everything is. I told you not to phone my friends, they don't want to be involved.'

'Can I see you for a minute, Christine, please?'

'No, you can't.' I slammed the phone down thoughtlessly. I was anxious to get away from the number they all knew.

Mandy took ages to get ready but she looked like her old self again, only her elaborate coiffure was delaying us. I had never liked those piles of pinned curls, I always wore my hair swinging free, but I was to be grateful for her attention to detail. Had she not pinned each and every one so laboriously we would have been halfway down the street with no cover at all when Johnny Edgecombe arrived. The

95

doorbell rang. Mandy looked out of the window and stopped me as I went to answer it.

Mandy asked me if she should let him in, and my answer was an unequivocal 'no'. It sounds heartless but at that moment all I wanted to do was rid myself of my past. All right, he had been a marvellous lover, but being trapped by possessive, violent men was not the life-style I was seeking from now on.

'She's gone to the hairdressers,' Mandy yelled out of the window. There was a mini-cab outside waiting for him.

'I want to come in,' Johnny shouted back stubbornly. 'I just want to talk to her.' Mandy may be a very good actress now but her performance that afternoon was not exactly subtle. Between yelling down at him, assuring him I was out, she kept glancing back at me for directions. He didn't have to be that clever to know I was there. I went to the window. He looked ghastly. His skin may have been black but he looked grey and dreadful.

'Johnny, please go away, there will be trouble if you stay. Have you got a gun?' I asked him.

'No. No,' he assured me. I went straight to the phone and phoned the police. In my eagerness to get back to town, using Mandy's bereavement as an excuse, I had looked for my gun at Brentwood, but it was missing. Suddenly Johnny was shooting at the door lock. Mandy and I flung ourselves on the floor and even then the sight of Mandy trying to wriggle under the bed for safety had us both giggling, hysterics I suppose.

I peered over the window sill to plead with him. He was waiting for me, and aimed straight up at me, the bullet lodging in the wall beside me. Mandy had now let the police know the address. I slithered down the stairs to close the entrance from the garage and after a while there was silence. Then we heard noises from the back garden and thought he was going to climb in through the bedroom. We knew the police were on their way but it seemed an eternity before I found the courage to sneak to the front window and discover that the mini-cab, and Johnny, had gone.

The use of guns in the street is still pretty rare in Britain but in 1962 a gun was headline material. The police and the press were on our doorstep almost simultaneously. Although it was Mandy's lethargic attitude to our shopping spree that had stopped us, or me at least, from being shot at while walking down the street, she should be forever grateful to me for my bullying that day. If the press had seen her looking as she had a couple of hours earlier she would never have forgiven herself. As it was the whole event sparked her to life again.

We were carted off to Marylebone Police Station for questioning and even I could see the great yawning maw ahead of me.

They had found the gun in the back garden, and they had also found Johnny Edgecombe pretty quickly. It was not going to take Johnny very long to tell them where the gun had come from – he was already a wanted man for Lucky's slashing, and I had conspired to keep him from the authorities. My name was in their files linked with Lucky Gordon's attack at Stephen's house, complete with mention of the fact that I had smoked dope and allowed myself to get into a situation of rape at knife-point. It wasn't difficult to deduce their opinion of a girl who got raped by one violent black man then went off to live with another. I was in trouble all right.

I telephoned Stephen from the station and was astounded by his reaction. I had expected his laughing, soothing voice. I had expected him to be as indulgent of my escapades as ever, to tell me all would be well. After all, hadn't he been fascinated by the slashing, titillated by my imprisonment and descriptions of Lucky's chopper, enchanted by the details of his enslavement? I thought he would be thrilled to know that there were crowds of journalists and photographers waiting outside for us. I was wrong.

'Tell Mandy to collect her things and get out,' he ordered. 'Take her to stay with you for a while.'

Mandy was boiling with indignation; not only had she been in a shooting incident and been asked some very awkward questions about how she earned her living, but she had paid her rent in advance. That really hurt.

The incident made headline news in all the papers the next day which wasn't surprising. It was a story that had everything. Black man, white girls, all the connotations of guns and violence, and all happening at the home of a man who was well known in society. They could drop almost as many names as Stephen. Of course the one name they wanted to drop, that of John Profumo, was impossible because of the libel laws. They had heard the rumours, knew of Stephen's reputation however inaccurately, knew that he was always seen around with pretty young girls, took them to parties where distinguished men and those of doubtful sexual character mixed, and that he was a great friend of a Russian diplomat. Grave doubts were being expressed all round about the competence of the Security Service.

All of this was quite beyond me. All I knew was that I did not want to stand up in court and admit that I had had sexual intercourse with two black men. The police had made it very clear that this time I stood no chance of dropping the charges. It is not a very pleasant thing to have to say about oneself but the slogan 'Black is Beautiful' was not yet invented, let alone accepted.

Without Stephen's support I felt lost. Then I remembered a friend and patient of his, a retired solicitor who had written a book called *A Man on Your Conscience* about Timothy Evans. His name was Michael Eddowes,

98

and he had driven me to my mother's home on several occasions. He knew all about Lucky and, only two weeks previously, had dropped me off at the end of the street in Brentwood where Johnny was hiding, though I imagine I hadn't told him why I was living in such a godforsaken place. I rang him and begged him to help me out with some advice. At the time I thought that all I needed was a good barrister who would stand up in court and shout 'Objection' if the defence asked me if I had slept with the accused. Michael came round to Great Cumberland Place immediately and tried to explain the facts to me. They were depressing.

'Look, Christine, the man will be fighting for his life, he is facing a very long sentence. He will tell the court he slashed Lucky to protect you and the details of that relationship will come out. Then they will want to know why a young girl living with an older man should need a gun, and how you acquired it. They might blame you for provoking both attacks and want to know how you came to be mixed up with such people in the first place.'

I told him that Stephen was insisting his name be kept out of the case – which I thought was unfair, as the trips to Paddington and that first purchase of marijuana had been his idea.

'Can you prove that, Christine?'

I remembered Lord d'Lazlo accompanying us to the Rio and said I supposed he could be called as a witness, but it seemed to me we were getting away from the point, which was to protect my name. What a hope! I was in deep and didn't know it.

Michael explained to me that he would have to know many more details of my life in order to prepare my defence. Being a friend of Stephen's he had heard Jack Profumo's name dropped fairly frequently the year before and, driving me to my mother's one weekend, had asked me if I still saw him. I had told him how angry I was that Jack had asked me to choose between himself and Stephen; of course I had chosen Stephen. Michael then asked me how well I knew Eugene and I told him I had had just the one fling, that it had actually happened the day I met Jack but it was quite unimportant.

'So you were seeing Lucky, John Profumo and Ivanov all at the same time? Did any of them ever go to the Rio club?'

'Ivanov may have gone with Stephen but I shouldn't think so, certainly never when I was there. Jack wouldn't have, he didn't like Stephen, and anyhow I wasn't "seeing" them all at the same time. Lucky was being a nuisance and Eugene tried to avoid me after that once. I can't see what this has got to do with anything.'

'It's all right, Christine, I'm just checking the facts. Now how about this question Ivanov asked you? About when the Americans were going to give the Germans the bomb?'

'No, that was Stephen, not Eugene, and Stephen was only joking, he wasn't serious, it was just part of the fun, making up that I had bewitched both of them. You know Stephen, he liked pretending that he was living with a very powerful lady who could change the world, it was that week's game, that's all.'

'Then why did you mention it?'

'I suppose I thought it was odd, silly, but dangerous. Anyhow I couldn't, and didn't ask – our relationship wasn't like that. I still can't see where this is leading. That was over a year ago and nothing to do with Johnny Edgecombe.'

'My advice to you, Christine, is to tell the police all about it. It's more important than you think – it may be of international importance. Anyhow I'll get in touch with you as soon as I've heard the charges. We'll work something out.'

He never telephoned me again but apparently had gone home and made notes. It was a confusing time and the exact chronology of events is difficult to recall, possibly because I turned to having a smoke like others turn to the bottle in times of stress. I know Bill Astor rang me to say that there were rumours that I was going to mention Profumo's name at the Edgecombe trial, that I was going to drag everyone, including himself, into it. Could he come round and talk to me?

Kim was visiting me and cooked us a frozen chicken pie. I bet that was the first time he had eaten such humble food. Over dinner I explained to him that my only concern was not upsetting my mum, and anyhow I couldn't see how it would help me to mention anyone's name, let alone his.

He assured me that if that was the case he would provide the best solicitor and barrister available and pay the costs himself. He treated the whole thing lightly and I began to relax. So did he. He never telephoned again either . . .

They say bad luck comes in threes (though I've never noticed good luck following suit) and the next thing was an almost hysterical phone call from my mum in Wraysbury. All I had dreaded her finding out about was there.

'It was terrible, Christine, a black man arrived at the door and all the neighbours could see.' The press had very kindly printed my mother's address in one of their articles, God knows who gave it to them, and now Lucky had turned up demanding to know where I was. 'I thought he was going to kill me, Chris, he wouldn't go away even though I told him you weren't here. I had to climb over the fence and hide next door. Then he went and sat on the hill till it was dark. I'm scared.'

'Don't worry, mum, he won't come back. It's me he's after.'

'What do you mean, don't worry? What's going on, Chris?'

'Oh mum, I'm sorry. Look, I'll get hold of some money and I'll get you out of there, I promise. I don't know what's going on either. He's mad, mum, I'm sure he'll be in prison soon.'

It was a rash promise and I didn't know how I was going to keep it but I loved her, I couldn't let her be frightened and, worse still, shamed. I rang the police and asked for protection, a plea that fell on unsympathetic, deaf ears. I changed the locks of the flat and only allowed Kim, Mandy, Nina Gadd and Paul Mann into the place. Paul was staying at Wimpole Mews with Stephen; the publicity was worrying him and he daren't have one of his girlfriends living there, much as he loathed having a man around the place. Somehow the dramas were getting too close to home. Stephen wanted to be in the front row of the stalls, not strutting on the stage.

The press were still hanging around, asking questions, trying to trap me, but quite frankly Mr Profumo's adultery was the least of my problems. I had worries of my own and, like anybody else, I aired them to all who would listen.

On Christmas Eve 1962 Paul Mann took me off to a party that some old friends from the Cabaret Club were holding. My notoriety over the shooting case had preceded me and that was how I was introduced to John Lewis, former MP for Bolton West. He seemed very sympathetic, and told me how much he understood my plight as he had sued a couple of newspapers for libel himself and consequently knew a great deal about the law. He listened very attentively to my troubles with Lucky and Johnny and to the fact that Stephen, in my hour of need, had deserted me. He seemed a good-hearted soul, fat and balding, with chubby chops, and he made me laugh. I felt secure and told him how disappointed I was in Michael Eddowes and Bill Astor, who seemed interested only in my affair with Profumo, which anyway had been over for ages and had nothing to do with my present troubles. Self pity made me eloquent and I had found a shoulder to cry on at last. He promised to introduce me to a solicitor after Christmas. Everything would be all right.

Nobody present at that party could have known that to the jovial little John Lewis I was the heaven-sent opportunity for revenge that he had been waiting for for over eight years. In 1954 he had won a divorce case against his wife, Joy. The hearing had lasted fifteen days and Stephen had given evidence for her. He hated Stephen's guts. The other information not known to me was that he was a friend of Michael Eddowes and of George Wigg, a Labour MP who distrusted Profumo. All of them wanted the present government out. I had just delivered the Christmas present of all time; the chance of personal revenge *and* a political powder keg all in one package.

I went off and enjoyed my Christmas, thinking that my only problem was how to keep my promise to my mum. When I turned up to make my commercial for Knight's Castile soap the director had turned to me and said: 'Aren't you the girl involved in that shooting and the black fella?'

When I said, 'Yes, that's true', the day's work was cancelled. They didn't want their nice clean white soap associated with the likes of me.

CHAPTER SIX

1963 began ominously. Stephen and I quarrelled. It was only the second time in all our years together. The first had been when Mandy and I were living at Comeragh Road and had gone to Cliveden for the weekend. I was having my affair with Tim Vigors and Mandy had gone to bed with Stephen, the only time she ever did. The next morning Mandy and I were jumping up and down on the old sofa, laughing at the noise the old springs made. We were behaving like kids (which we were) when Stephen got irritable and shouted at us. I burst into tears at his anger and we had hitch-hiked back to London.

This time it was I who shouted at Stephen. We were coming back from a New Year's Eve party, and the weather was dreadful, with deep snow and ice on the roads. The car was only a two seater and Kim and some bloke were crammed into the back.

'She'll have to get out and take a taxi,' Stephen screamed.

'No she won't!' It was my turn to scream. 'How dare you suggest leaving her all alone? If she gets out so do I.'

Stephen was shocked. It was the first time I had ever stood up for someone against him. We got out and he drove off. I felt that same light-hearted sense of freedom I always did whenever I ran from something oppressive.

It was a bad omen. Had we known that by the next New Year one of us would be dead and buried and the other one in jail we would have clung to each other and never let go. We didn't and our fateful year, our separation for ever had begun.

John Lewis was as good as his word and rang me, inviting me to his house. He told me that Frank Sinatra and Ava Gardner had stayed there once and I was duly impressed. His place had a large sitting-dining room, a morning room, a vast kitchen and an office. 'I keep dossiers on a great many people in there,' he indicated. It seemed reasonable, he was a powerful man.

He, too, asked a lot of questions about Jack, Ivanov and Stephen's joking suggestion about the bomb. He asked too about our disappointing little MI5 man. Patiently I pointed out that it had nothing to do with the shooting case. Only belatedly did I discover that he was taping all our conversations.

Ridiculously, too, he made a pass at me, offering me money to sleep with him. I will never know whether that was to be another taped trap so that he could prove in court that I was a whore, because I had no interest in taking up his proposition (I imagine that particular tape got lost or recycled) but it led to another hysterical scene. He frightened me because he kept insisting that everything about my past would come out in court and that if I denied it I would be put away for perjury.

At one moment he stormed out of his office and I locked the door behind him. 'Right,' I thought, 'if you've got a dossier on Stephen and me I'll find it.' Of course I couldn't, I didn't know where to start looking, and when he started banging and shouting at the door I let him in.

He was now quite mad, telling me there was no way he would let me go unless I made love to him.

'You will have to shoot me first,' he declared and actually handed me a gun. The whole thing was absurd. There was I, seeking his advice on the Johnny Edgecombe case, and this respectable middle-aged gent who was supposed to be helping me out was playing the drama queen.

'Go on, it's loaded,' he insisted.

So I did. I aimed it at him and clicked the trigger. It wasn't loaded but I will never forget his face.

'You would have shot me,' he stammered in disbelief. That little game was over and he let me go.

So now I had no one. No Stephen, no Michael Eddowes, no Bill Astor and no John Lewis. I didn't understand what was going on but in their limited way Paul Mann, Nina Gadd and Mandy did. Their interest in the whole intrigue was not political but financial. They recognised that I was, as they say, sitting on a gold mine. And one in which everyone could have a share. And why not? Hadn't everyone already?

Their arguments were very practical. I had no money, I was still being threatened by Lucky, the press were anxious to talk to me and would pay me. I could use the money to retain a lawyer of my own. There might even be enough to get mum away till it all blew over. Nina brought a 'friend' round to advise me who asked me if I had any proof of these rumours. I remembered the letters Jack had sent me, rummaged through my belongings and found them. The 'friend' was a reporter from the *Sunday Pictorial*. The one I produced was the one Jack had written cancelling a date the same day that he had been cautioned by Sir Norman Brook, though I knew nothing of that. It read:

'Darling

In great haste and because I can get no reply on your phone——

Alas something's blown up tomorrow night and I can't therefore make it. I'm terribly sorry especially as I leave the next day for various trips and then a holiday so won't be able to see you again until sometime in September.

Christine leaving court.

P. MANEVY

Stephen Ward leaving Marylebone Magistrates Court.

P. MANEVY

Christine with her first husband, James Levermore and their son Jimmy.

Christine with her son Jimmy aged 3.

Christine with appropriate reading matter.
BLACK STAR

LORD DENNING'S
REPORT

A recent portrait.

Blast it. Please take great care of yourself and don't run away.

Love J.

P.S. I'm writing this 'cos I know you're off for the day tomorrow and I want you to know before you go if I still can't reach you by phone.'

It wasn't exactly how Dante wrote to his Beatrice but it was written on War Office headed paper.

I weakened a bit the following morning but Mandy was firm. We set off to Fleet Street together, with Jack's letters in my handbag. It was all very complicated, with lots of reporters coming and going, taking notes, and assuring me that everything was going to be fine. Since there was no way they could mention Jack's name, the story was going to be about a model and a Minister, MI5 and men in high places. I also told them how everyone else had let me down and the only thing that seemed to interest them was Stephen asking me to get Jack to tell about when the Americans were going to pass on to Germany the information about the bomb. They agreed with me that it must have been a joke, and promised they would pay me £1,000 in all when I signed the story and in the meantime here was a couple of hundred to be getting on with.

Mandy and I felt very pleased with our morning's work as we left the building. But as with John Lewis, I had no idea that once again I had just become an instrument of revenge.

The press were engaged in their own war with the government. The Vassall Tribunal was under way and two journalists were being pressured to reveal their sources of information on the story that had led to the exposure of a spy in the Navy. Lord Carrington, then First Lord of the Admiralty, had known that there was a leak for eighteen months. My story might be very useful for discrediting the government even more. When the two journalists were jailed Fleet Street grimly set about its new task.

Again several things happened at once. Stephen moved out of Wimpole Mews and into Peter Rachman's old flat in Bryanston Square. Mandy was beside herself with rage.

'The bastard,' she screamed. 'Nearly everything in that place belongs to me, he's just taken over all my possessions, my record player, my fridge, and I can't even get in there.'

I tried to calm her down.

'Look, I'm sure it's only temporary till all this blows over. It's just to keep his picture out of the papers, you can't blame him, it must be very bad for his business.'

'Well, I think he's a creep and I don't know why you're standing up for him, Chris. He may have been a friend of yours once but don't think he is any longer because he isn't,' she added spitefully. 'Don't think he's going around sticking up for you 'cos he isn't.'

Kim joined in, agreeing with Mandy, darkly hinting that it was about time I started to understand what was going on and that Stephen was washing his hands of me. I wouldn't believe them, Stephen would never let me down. We had made up our little tiff, he had always been my protector, it was he who had explained everything to the police when Lucky had attacked me and sent me out of the room to spare me. Or was it? Slowly Kim and Mandy persuaded me that Stephen would do anything to save his own skin. They insisted that Kim should ring him and I was to listen in to the things Stephen was saying about me. We stood with our heads together, Kim doing the talking. Stephen rose to the bait.

'I'm absolutely furious with her, I'm ashamed and disgusted with her behaviour, what with her blacks and her drugs, she's got no consideration for other people and now she's dragged me into it, she's ruining my business. I never know what she'll do next, the silly girl, she's completely scatterbrained, all I have ever done is try and look after her and now she repays me like this. . . . '

108

'That's lies, Stephen, and you know it!' I shouted as I snatched the phone from Kim. 'You know it was you who took me to those places in the first place *and* made me buy the drugs, it was you who gave the pusher our address, and if the police ask me about it I'm going to tell them the truth . . .'

Stephen had slammed the phone down. I looked from Kim to Mandy, hurt and horrified. Kim tried to look sympathetic but it came out more 'I told you so'. Mandy was well worked up and already dialling back to him to tell him he had no right to be in her flat, since Peter had meant to leave it to her. Stephen laughed straight back at her, telling her that without Peter she'd have had nothing and had had a good run for her money anyhow. In any case, he pointed out, the flat now belonged to Peter's wife and there was nothing she could do about that.

My hurt was busy turning into rage. How dare he say he had tried to look after me? Who else had made me pretend to be a whore down a dark street in Paddington, had encouraged me to go to bed with Profumo, made me get girls for him?

Stephen Ward had just made two very dangerous little enemies.

We were both still seething when Detective Sergeant Burrows called round to tell us that Johnny Edgecombe's trial would be held sometime early in February and that we would both be needed as witnesses. Detective Burrows seemed a nice, safe, comfortable man, and over a cup of tea I felt that I had at last met someone I could trust. At least a policeman wouldn't pounce on me and he must know as much about the law as all those people who had given me empty promises. I asked him the question that none of my 'advisers' had bothered to answer, the only one that concerned me.

'I can't get into trouble over this case, can I? I mean, he attacked me, yet everyone makes it look like my fault.'

109

'Of course not,' the detective replied soothingly. 'You're only a witness. Why, what's bothering you?'

'People are saying that I enticed Lucky Gordon and then set Johnny up but it wasn't like that. It was Stephen who took me down to Paddington in the first place, and made me go and buy some pot, that's how I met Lucky.'

'Yes, it's all Stephen's fault,' chipped in Mandy, anxious to add her two-pennorth. 'He's a very wicked influence on young girls, I should think he's had every girl in London at some time, he picks them up for a while then drops them. He threw me out after the shooting and now he's taken my flat, the one I lived in with Peter Rachman and now all this has happened he won't have anything to do with us.'

Our moral indignation was well under way now. When Burrows asked us what else Dr Ward got up to it all poured out easily; his fascination with whips and high heels, picking up young girls for sex and taking them to Cliveden where he had a cottage on Lord Astor's estate, going to orgies. For extra measure we threw in that we understood he had become completely dirty and associated with very rough prostitutes. I went on to explain that the men I had turned to for help were only interested in my affair with John Profumo and the Russian.

'So in the end I just had to go to the newspapers to sell my story so I can afford a solicitor.'

'And what story was that?'

'That I have had an affair with John Profumo, the War Minister, and with Eugene Ivanov who is with the Russian Embassy. I gave them a letter Jack wrote to me on War Office headed paper to prove I am telling the truth. They've given me two hundred pounds and they will give me another eight when they've written it all and I sign it.'

'How did you come to meet all these people?'

'Stephen introduced me, I was living with him and they were his friends.'

'And we told them about the bomb.' Mandy again, making sure the policeman understood the importance of our story. His face was impassive as he closed his notebook but his heart must have been beating like a drum. He had stumbled across a bomb himself.

If Mandy and I felt we had cooked Stephen's goose, there was no pleasure in it for me. We had spoken badly of him, Mandy because of her possessions and I because he had betrayed me. There were even stories going around that he was trying to have me put inside as a drug addict. Our lovely, laughing, spontaneous relationship was over, we were all fighting for survival.

The curious thing is that we had no interest in cooking Profumo's goose. He had never done me any harm, and I intended him none. All he represented to me now was money. If people wanted to pay me to tell the truth, that was OK by me. I needed it and they had plenty. So Greed and Spite shook hands with Political Deviousness and we were all doomed.

Stephen soon got to hear that I had placed my story with the *Sunday Pictorial*, that as soon as I signed I would receive money and that it would be published after the Edgecombe case. The *Pictorial* had assured me that the name of the Minister involved would not be printed (due to the libel laws) so I couldn't really understand the fuss. But I knew there was a lot of activity going on from Paul Mann who seemed to be in with everyone. He told me that Stephen had sought powerful legal advice, had lunched with Bill Astor and Profumo, and had had a second, private meeting with Jack. It turned out later that Profumo had gone straight to the Security Service in the hope that they would slap a D notice (a memo issued to editors suggesting that the information before them should not be published in the national interest) on the *Pictorial*. Many years later I learned that Stephen's hopes had been even higher and

111

typically more dramatic; that MI5 would get windy and arrange for me to meet with an accident. Both sets of hopes were dashed.

Stephen rang the *Pictorial* to inform them that they were making a great mistake, that I was a notoriously unreliable young woman who had got into bad company, that the letter they had was nothing more than a polite note regretting that Profumo could not accept an invitation to a cocktail party, that he was quite sure I was making it all up. Fleet Street was by no means as sure. They had my descriptions of the inside of the house in Regents Park and of the mascot on the bonnet of the car that Jack had used when he took me for that first drive. They knew it must have belonged to Mr John Hare, the Aviation Minister, but they were nervous of printing. Stephen suggested that he had a better human-interest story about Christine Keeler and the dangers young girls coming to London alone to seek their fortunes could run into. That lunch with Bill and Jack must have been quite a summit conference too.

On the first Saturday afternoon in February, Profumo's solicitor came to ask me about the details of my contract with the paper. I told him the truth about my brief affair with Jack but I suppose he was duty bound to believe his client. I got the distinct impression that I was being offered compensation if I was prepared not to sign, but they would prefer not to deal with me direct and offered me instead the name of a reliable lawyer. When he left I had another distinct feeling – that I had done something very wrong and was in it up to my neck.

When Paul came back I poured out my fears and the news of my visitor.

'Relax, Christine,' he said. 'It just sounds like they want to buy you off, and why not? It doesn't matter to you where the money comes from, just so long as you get it. I think I'd better handle it this time, I don't think the *Pictorial* deal is nearly enough. You should have a solicitor of your own,

112

you are dealing with very powerful people, you could be facing a libel case.'

'But the paper promised not to mention names and anyhow Jack's solicitor said he would find me one.' Even as I was bleating my protests I was remembering the way the others, Eddowes, Lewis and Astor, had treated me. Why should Jack Profumo's recommendation be any more reliable?

When Paul told me the name of a solicitor that Stephen's counsel had suggested, an ex-pupil of his, I meekly accepted; Stephen was still a great influence on my life.

I can honestly look back at this period in my life and think I was going gently mad. I was out of my depth. The interview with Mr Gerald Black, the solicitor chosen by Stephen's counsel, did not go well. I explained my financial difficulties, including finding a new home for my mum. He was not sympathetic.

'Your story can do a lot of damage,' he said. I told him I knew that now but that had not been the intention in the first place. I had only come to realise the value of my information from the interest shown by others who already knew the gossip and had used the Edgecombe shooting as a chance to revive old whispers. I was three weeks away from my twenty-first birthday and was beginning to learn at last. But not fast enough to outwit trained lawyers. Oh, it was all delicately conducted between them. First there was the refutation that Mr Profumo was willing to buy my silence. I wasn't the one who was asking. But Dr Ward's counsel might be able to organise a recompense for loss of earnings (meaning the feature), some money for my parents' home and enough to get me out of the country for an extended holiday after the Edgecombe trial. They did not care to explain where Stephen was going to get the money from but offered me £3,000. I said I would probably need five. It was agreed. Five.

Mr Black gave me fifty for my immediate expenses and I

113

was to return on the morrow for the rest. Paul Mann answered the phone to the *Pictorial* all evening saying that I was unavailable for the signing. I went to collect my money the next day. Mr Black handed me an envelope.

'There you are, five hundred pounds, no sorry four-fifty really as we've already had fifty of it.'

I couldn't believe it. 'But you agreed five thousand yesterday with their solicitor.'

Adding insult to injury, Mr Black proceeded to dictate the terms on which I could accept the money. First I must break with Mandy, secondly place my parents in a hotel for the duration, thirdly promise to leave the country as soon as the case was over for at least a month.

'When you return,' he assured me with a cynical smile, 'you will be looked after, your future will be secure. If you do not agree, I wish to point something out to you. You may have noticed a girl sitting in the outer office . . . ' I had indeed noticed a poor, hunched thing of a person sitting out there. 'She, too, once sold a story to the newspapers about friends she had in the Establishment, look at her now. It could happen to you.'

Rage either tears people to pieces or lends them dignity. I was lucky on that day that mine took the latter form. Later I learned that it had been a filthy trick, that Profumo was already taking advice from the DPP about blackmail threats. As it was my dignity extended itself to informing Mr Black that he could shove his money right up the same high places his friends came from, along with his cheap threats. I was going to sign, publish and be damned. I was too.

Lord Denning was kind enough to believe half of what I said and 95% of the lawyers' accounts. Mr Black may have made a slight error of judgement due to his lack of experience. What about mine?

Right bang in the middle of their fervid activity came the

news that Johnny's trial was to be postponed; the mini-cab driver who had witnessed the shooting and been forced to help Johnny escape, had been taken ill with a heart attack from which he later died, I wonder what his evidence would have been? How many names had Johnny mentioned on his way to and from Brentwood in his manic state? Probably the man was too scared to listen or remember but it did give rise to a reference in a newspaper to Lucky Profumo.

The *Sunday Pictorial* decided to ditch me in favour of Dr Ward's revelations about the perils of young girls in London; neither the police nor the press were interested in me any more. Paul and Kim were planning a holiday in Spain and I listened with envy, as I am sure Paul meant me to. Without doubt he was a slippery number, listening to the lawyers' avowed worries that I would not appear in court, meeting all Stephen's friends; I think he got the message. It is still difficult to assess who wanted me out of the way at the time of the resumed trial in March, whether it was Eddowes, Lewis and George Wigg in order to draw attention to the fact that Profumo might be a security risk, or whether it was Bill, Jack and Stephen trying to keep their noses clean.

Certainly we had no money when we set out. I was easily persuaded – an impulse was an impulse as far as I was concerned. We bundled into Paul's Jaguar with less than a hundred quid between us though Paul said he had an insurance cheque that he could cash in Spain when we got there. We drove like bats out of hell all the way to a small fishing village outside Alicante and found ourselves a little villa for thirty bob a week. All I knew was that I never wanted to hear of a title, a posh lawyer's voice or a threatening West Indian one ever again. But I wanted to see the papers just to know the whole thing was over and done with.

Every day Paul left the villa to make a phone call about

his insurance money. Every day he came back without any British newspapers – we were out of the tourist season, he explained.

We met a couple of Spanish bullfighters who invited us to a party. We accepted but didn't realise until we were well on the way in their Aston Martin car that the party was five hundred miles away in Madrid. There again, what's a few more miles, we thought as we drove through the night and arrived the following evening in time for a luxurious bath and a party at some American's apartment.

We hadn't enough money to stay in Madrid and planned to get back to the village by bus, first calling on our American host for coffee and farewells. The American made us welcome, then one of them said, half-curiously, 'You're Christine Keeler, aren't you?'

I assumed he had caught my name the night before and nodded vaguely.

'Hey, I've been reading about you in the *International Herald Tribune*, all about your name coming up in Parliament and everything.'

'What? What on earth are you talking about, me and Parliament?' I thought he must be confused about the December shooting headlines.

'I've got the papers upstairs, come and have a look.'

We all rushed up the stairs and there it was. An article about me being a missing witness at Johnny Edgecombe's trial, about how I was associated with Dr Ward and knew many distinguished people in London. That the Opposition, in their concern that there could be yet another espionage scandal brewing, had asked questions about me in the House. It also stated that the Secretary of State for War, Mr John Profumo, had denied any knowledge of my disappearance and of 'any impropriety' in connection with me. It was accompanied by one of my modelling pictures.

'What's impropriety?' was my first question.

'Screwing' was the terse reply.

Suddenly there was a very funny atmosphere in the room. For once I kept my mouth shut. I looked to Paul for guidance.

'I had better phone the British Consul and find out what's going on,' he said grimly.

The American offered Paul the use of his phone but Paul decided that it would be safer to use an outside one in case I was in trouble and the phones got tapped. If it seemed over-dramatic I didn't notice because I was too scared. I had no idea what the punishment for not turning up at a court of law might be.

Of poor Jack Profumo I thought nothing, because I also had no idea of the enormity of what he had done.

The American invited us to stay until Paul returned and after a while excused himself, saying that he was off to the bullfight. Kim and I thought this very kind of him until he returned half an hour later with three American reporters and a black man. I didn't like the look of any of them and firmly denied my identity. Kim insisted that we were just a couple of tourists but they were not convinced and tried to persuade me to come out and have a coffee across the road. They all stood up, with the black man leading the way, opening the door for me. Well, I may have been dumb, but by now I wasn't that daft and could see how the trap was set. There would be a photographer outside just waiting to snap Christine Keeler emerging from a block of flats in Madrid with yet another black man. Great, just what I needed. Paul phoned and I explained the situation I was in.

'Right, don't say anything at all. Get out as fast as you can and meet me at the Palace Hotel.' I was so relieved to hear from him I forgot to ask him what the British Consul had said.

It was time to play docile again. These reporters weren't the only ones with skills.

117

'Look, I'll give you a story but I must insist on no photographs at the moment.' They agreed willingly, anything for a story, and wrote a message on a card. 'I'll take it downstairs myself, just so we all know where we stand,' I told them firmly. I checked it out, the card was a typical press trick to put my mind at ease. 'Go back to the office, will contact later' it read. It meant the fella would be round the corner or further up the street when they had persuaded me that all was clear. I pushed it under the door. Apparently satisfied I asked my American host to take Kim to a bar where I could meet them later. After they had gone I allowed the three pressmen to settle down, their notepads and pens poised.

'Well, about this coffee?' I said, and I was through the door and into the lift before they could rise from their seats. I hailed a cab to the Palace Hotel, expecting to find Paul there waiting to pay for it. No Paul, so I had to borrow money from the barman, order a drink and some cigarettes and wait. No call, no Paul, and I was getting worried except for the fact there was an American giving me the eye. He paid my bill and offered to drive me to meet Kim. No sign of anyone, Kim, Paul or our American host, but plenty of signs from my companion that he was anxious to get us booked into a hotel room. I was frightened now, not of him, but of possibly being hunted by Interpol or some such organisation. I needed somewhere safe and the best place was the authorities. I told him to drive me to the police.

Spain in 1963 was not the El Fish and Chips place it is now. When I arrived at the station nobody could speak English. I tried to explain that I was the missing Miss Keeler and they very obligingly looked up Hotel Keeler thinking I had lost my address. Finally they found an interpreter who tried to phone the Consulate. It was out of order like most of their communications system and they gallantly offered me the choice between a bed in a cell or a couple of chairs in the reception area. I plumped for the chairs, the Spanish prisons being quite famous for their excess of creature occupants rather than comforts.

The police were actually very sweet to me and I had to rush to their defence when the British Consul arrived after breakfast demanding to know why I had been held. I told him of my predicament (of which he should have been well aware) and he told me he could only send me back by train.

'But that'll take days. What about my mum? She'll be worried sick at all those stories.' Actually I was trying to twist his arm, I had sent my mum a card from the village to say I was having a lovely rest away from it all. Somewhere in the middle of all the officialdom, the arguments and the noise, Paul arrived with the news that there were ten representatives from the *Daily Express* waiting for me at a hotel with a contract. They would also fly me back to London. The British Consul was happy to agree and save the government expense. I should have kicked Paul Mann where it hurt there and then the way he had deserted me the night before, but the thought of instant cash banished any such thoughts, and Kim was already there.

I was round there like a shot to sign a contract for two grand. The first thing they wanted to know was whether I had slept with Profumo. I denied it. I knew they knew the gossip, how could they fail to after Stephen's around-the-town chatter? But after the *Sunday Pictorial* experience I knew that I had ventured on to very dangerous ground. I had been bullied and threatened by some very high-powered people since then, I knew that the politicians and lawyers worked hand in glove and that the people out there, including the press, were trying to manipulate me for their own ends. I wasn't averse to making money but if Jack had said there had been nothing between us I was better off honouring his decision. It must have been the first time I really thought about him as a person, someone who had much to lose. After all, what had it been? A few afternoons in bed a long time ago. Even then I thought more in terms of him losing his wife (though, like all married men, he had suggested that she would not be unduly concerned about a little unfaithfulness. After all, he reasoned, she was an actress.) I never thought about a government.

Years later, when Sarah Macmillan became a close friend of mine, she told me that her father, who was Prime Minister at the time of Profumo's statement to the House, could not abide the thought of adultery ever since he had discovered that his wife, Lady Dorothy, had had an affair with Lord Boothby. In those circumstances it was reasonable for John not to want to own up and for Macmillan not to want to know. But the *Daily Express* were gunning for Macmillan. While I had been away they had run a front page with a picture of John and Valerie on one side of the page and me on the other. The headline 'War Minister Shock' ran right across the page with the story that he had offered the Prime Minister his resignation. Under my picture a caption identified me as a missing witness in an attempted murder case. To the unknowing reader it must all have looked very innocent.

This had all happened a week before the *Express* had found me, though I soon began to suspect that some of the events of the last two weeks were not half as accidental as they appeared. Any glimmer of ego and stardom that I may have felt at the sight of my picture on the front page of a national newspaper was soon knocked out of me by the treatment I received while they worked on my story. There were now thirteen of us confined to a tiny flat, there were photographers climbing on to the roof opposite trying to snatch pictures, the doorbell and phone were ringing incessantly. I was not even allowed to go to the loo without a reporter standing outside . . . not a dainty situation after two weeks on Spanish food. Paul was busy managing everything. Until a nice photographer got Kim on one side.

'Listen, Kim, you know he's got fifty per cent of that contract with Christine, don't you?'

Kim told me straight away – we had had enough of Paul's connivings. I wasn't having that. The whole thing began to look very dodgy indeed. The impetuous jaunt, Paul's mysterious phone calls, never a sight of an English paper, and ending up in Madrid with all the papers searching for me? And with a contract? No.

We were on our way to the next hideout when I tackled Paul.

'I think you should have 25% of the money I am going to receive, Paul.' I was all innocence and generosity. He was evasive and said we should discuss it later. We did. Through a locked door. There was a bit of a scuffle outside as the *Express* men retrieved the old contract from Paul and the new percentage was agreed. The newspaper arranged for Kim and Paul to return to our village to collect our clothes and passports and then to meet us at a hotel in Valencia – we met and our passports were exchanged. I said to Paul, 'I'm going to fix you,' and we both deserted him, his face was a picture. Kim was used as a decoy for our return to London. The journey was pure madness. There were crowds when we changed planes at Orly, flash bulbs everywhere, the same when we got to London. I couldn't believe what was happening. It was only when I got to the hotel that the *Express* had booked me into that I began to understand. I had insisted that part of the contract included my mum and dad being there.

Mum was in as much of a flutter as I was. She had had a terrible time. She had kept all the newspapers for me and while I looked at them she told me she had been besieged in her own home. It all came out in a garbled rush.

'Oh Chris, you remember that man Michael Eddowes who used to drive you home? Well he came round just after

121

Mandy had left . . . Then Mandy came round with two reporters. I let her in because she's a friend of yours. She said "Come on, Julie, tell me where Christine is". Well, I'd got your postcard but I couldn't think why she wanted to know so urgently. Then she said "You've got to tell me, they said they'll give me £70 for letting them know where she is.'

If mum hadn't been in such a state I would have laughed.

'And then that Michael Eddowes, he was ranting away. He offered me money, he didn't want to know where you were, he just kept shouting "I want the government out, out, out." I didn't want his money, then he started to threaten us, saying we could be shot from the hill behind the house. He said he knew all about what you had been up to with the Russians, selling secrets, and you'd be sent to prison for treason and being a spy and he said he would give us £30,000 if we'd confirm it. I told him we didn't want his money and he said we'd be shot alongside you. Oh, Chris, what's going on?'

I wanted to say 'the world's gone barmy', then she mentioned that Nina Gidd had been round too with reporters. I thought of these friends since the shooting, Paul, Eddowes, Lewis, Astor and Mandy, and I felt sick.

I read the reports of Johnny Edgecombe's case. Somehow the poor mini-cab driver's death didn't seem half as important as my absence. Johnny was sentenced to seven years' imprisonment for possessing a firearm with intent to endanger life. They acquitted him of doing Lucky Gordon grievous bodily harm, and of attempting to do the same to me. They also acquitted him of having an offensive weapon. Quite right too. A few days later I had to make an appearance at the Old Bailey to convey my abject apologies to the court.

No one likes appearing in court. It is nerve racking even for the innocent. I knew by now it was a mere formality and

I was flanked by a couple of *Express* reporters, but I was in the news and a crowd had gathered. I had become some sort of a freak. As I got out of the taxi I looked up the steps. And there, at the top, was Lucky Gordon. I lost my cool and tried to scramble back into the cab. Lucky was shouting for all to hear.

'I love that girl, I love that girl!' he screamed. Five policemen rushed at him and there was a terrible scene, all thoroughly snapped. Someone had set me up again.

I was fined forty pounds.

CHAPTER SEVEN

AND THAT, I thought, was the end of that.

My ordeal had lasted more than three months but I would probably end up as a nine days' wonder. I went to stay with Paula Hamilton-Marshall at her flat in Devonshire Street. She was the only person I could trust, the others had all let me down. It was going to be the quiet life for me from now on.

But there were other forces at work, two in fact: the police force and the Security Service. Their chiefs met up with the Home Secretary to discuss Mr Profumo's Statement to the Commons and to pool the information they had collected. They came to the conclusion that there was not enough evidence to charge Stephen Ward under the Official Secrets Act but as they had received several anonymous letters alleging that he lived off the immoral earnings of girls they would investigate his sex life.

I am sure it was all done with gentlemanly officialdom, but I have always been convinced that somewhere around that time someone issued instructions to the effect of 'Get Ward and Get Keeler.' We had embarrassed the government and they didn't like it. The police investigations began immediately.

Although the Security Service was convinced that there had been no threat to the country there were members of the Opposition who had no wish to let the whole thing slip. Mr George Wigg was not an admirer of the War Minister and he was in possession of the facts via the tapes John

Lewis had made of my side of the story in January. He passed these on to Harold Wilson, then the Leader of the Opposition, who in turn passed some of the information to the Prime Minister. As the Opposition was only interested in the security aspect no mention was made of Profumo's sexual activities. Mr Macmillan suavely replied that he was happy to accept the advice of the Security Service that there had been no danger to the nation.

Meanwhile the police were back on my doorstep, this time with veiled threats that if I did not co-operate with them I could be facing charges as a spy. So we went over the saga of Stephen suggesting I ask Jack about the bomb and each time I told it the idea that it had only been a joke became thinner and thinner.

Although I had come to know Detective Sergeant Burrows and Inspector Herbert quite well over the previous couple of months, I felt uneasy enough to ring Stephen about this new development. He brushed my fears aside nonchalantly and suggested I came round for the evening as he had a film producer there.

The man's name was John Nash and he was going to make a film about me in Germany. Stephen was going to help with the screenplay and they wanted me to star in it. They offered me £3000 and 5% of the profits. I was a bit dubious – somehow all my attempts at fame and fortune seemed to go wrong – but Stephen persuaded me and I signed there and then. Throughout the evening I was aware things were different between Stephen and myself now. He still called me 'little baby' but it didn't ring true; there was a lack of trust between us that couldn't be restored.

Burrows and Herbert were round the next day asking when I had last seen Stephen, and I guessed then that I was being watched. They had with them a plan of Profumo's house, and pointed out how easy it would have been for me to enter his office while he was in the bathroom. It went on endlessly. Who had suggested we went there? Had it been Ivanov's idea? Why didn't Jack like Stephen? Had I told Stephen the layout of the house? And always back to when Stephen had asked me to find out when the Americans were going to give Germany the nuclear secrets.

Then it was back to Jack. How many times had we been to bed? Had Jack ever brought any papers with him? It was useless to try to explain to them that he did not come round for a polite cup of tea and a chat, and I bitterly regretted having been so forthcoming with Burrows on his first visit. The mask of courtesy had disappeared and my interrogations now took place in a windowless room at the station with all the classic techniques of the Gestapo. Inspector Herbert would bark questions at me, not allowing me to finish a sentence, explain, or even think. Then, when I began to get bolshie, Burrows would bring me a cup of tea and gently start all over again. They couldn't believe that Stephen and I had lived and slept together, yet had never screwed; every time I had to repeat how Stephen had phrased his question about the bomb they would ask if it was before or after intercourse. They always interviewed me at night, mistakenly thinking that being tired I might let something slip. But this was foolish of them really, as I had spent years sleeping all morning and staying up all night. Nevertheless it was dreary and draining to leave the station at four a.m. knowing they would be calling for me the next day. The blank walls were depressing, the hard chair made me ache and the harsh light made me tired. One day they started on a different tack. My finances.

'Why haven't you bought any new clothes, Christine? You've had money from the newspapers, what have you done with it?'

I told them that I had paid off some bills and put the rest in the bank, that I didn't often buy clothes and that as I was staying with Paula all I needed was a bit of cash for cigarettes and odds and ends like false eyelashes.

'So what have you done with the rest of the money?' I looked blank. 'The money you have received over the years. Come on, Christine, you must have been receiving large sums of money, the newspapers haven't been your only source of income, we know that. It's very clever of you not to flaunt it around but don't forget we have the powers to make a search and we'll soon find it.'

I was scared now, not because I had any money hidden but because I thought they were referring to the money men had paid me for my services and I knew they wouldn't deal with that leniently.

'Or have they been keeping it in another country for you?'

'They?'

'The people who have been paying you for information, Christine.'

Relief and indignation at the accusation that I would betray my country made my anger rise up in me and they let me go. But I was back again the next day. They started to ask about Bill Astor, how well I knew him, how many times I had been to Cliveden and whether I had had sex with him. Then it was:

'How about the time you shared a flat in Comeragh Road with Mandy Rice-Davies?' I couldn't think how they had found that piece of information or why it was important. They then started asking the names of every man I had met through Stephen and whether I had screwed them. Just in case any of them had Russian connections, they assured me. If it hadn't been so awful it would have been laughable. Apart from the fact that I couldn't remember half the names, most of Stephen's callers were so old I doubted if they could get it up, let alone tackle a lively youngster like me. It wouldn't have crossed their minds.

But I began to get the gist of things when they cunningly

took me into their confidence. They had been keeping an eye on Stephen's activities for eleven years, they told me. They knew all about how he used young girls for his own ends, to get in with people in positions of power.

After that they made me make a list of all the men who had ever given me money. It was useless to explain that I had often borrowed money from friends. I had to sign a statement declaring whether or not I had had sex with each name mentioned. My bad memory did me a good service at this point and many were left out. I made just the one error, and that would turn out to be very damning: that Stephen had brought a friend, Charles, round to the house once, that I had screwed him, and that some time afterwards Stephen had asked me to go round to Charles' house in Green Street and borrow some money.

When I got home that dawn my mind was confused with a million doubts. I had also been asked about my sudden departure for Spain. Had the suggestion come from Paul Mann? Had he been seeing Stephen? I tried to review the events of the past few years in the light of what they had told me. Was it possible that Stephen had been a spy all along? I remembered his reply when I had expressed doubts about Ivanov and he had said that there was money in it. But Stephen never had any money. Then I remembered Paul's odd behaviour in Spain. It was he who had told me that my evidence couldn't be essential, that the case was cut and dried. Could Stephen have planted that thought in Paul's mind? But that had been for money, it couldn't be a cover-up for a spy ring. Perhaps for the first time, I began to see that Stephen was indeed strange, that I had lived an abnormal life under his influence, that his reassuring ethics were wrong after all, that he had used his girl-friends to get in with people. As my mind raced on I even began to wonder if his beloved Vickie Martin's death had been an accident after all.

I also began to find out that I wasn't the only one being

128

interrogated. Every woman and many men associated with Stephen were being questioned and the queries were centring on his sexual associations and on money rather than any Russian connections. Women were being asked whether they had ever screwed a man Stephen had introduced them to and if they had ever given Stephen money. Some very distinguished gentlemen had to face similar enquiries. Girls with convictions for prostitution were coerced into giving the right answers.

One night I was so worried I rang Stephen to warn him that there was something very nasty going on. He scoffed at my fears and told me it was all in my imagination, then asked me round so that we could get together and write a book to go with the film. As I had by then seen the script, in which he came out whiter than white, I declined his offer.

I think he must have been going mad at the time because I later discovered that he had stepped up his activities and really was playing host at Bryanston Mews to various men and inviting established whores along for everyone's enjoyment. The awful thing was that he now really needed the money – what with the shooting scandal and the police follow-up his practice was almost at a standstill. Still, he must have checked out my fears and decided that perhaps it wasn't all imagination because he then rang the Prime Minister's Private Secretary to demand an audience. It was granted but Stephen, the great bridge player, played his cards wrong. Ever so subtly he indicated to the Private Secretary that unless the police were called off his back he might find himself in the intolerable position of having to refute Mr Profumo's statement to the House, at least about his relationship with Miss Keeler. The heavy hint appearing to go unremarked, he wrote in a similar vein to the Home Secretary deploring that his protection of Profumo's good name should have led the police to take up their present line of enquiry.

The Home Secretary informed him the next day that the

police were not under his jurisdiction. He had also sent letters containing a brief version of the contents to the newspapers but they decided not to print, so he applied to Harold Wilson for help, stating quite firmly that he had every intention of clearing his own name. But Stephen was running against the big boys now and in true blue fashion they closed ranks. Wilson recognised the ammunition he had in his hand but did not lift one finger to help Stephen.

But I was barely aware of these happenings, since I was now back in trouble on my own. Manu, my Persian boyfriend of two years back, the one I had been so disgracefully in love with, had gone to the police with the tale of my delivering letters to the Russian Embassy. I had forgotten all about them but now I had to answer questions about them. What were their contents? I didn't know because I hadn't read them. Were they notes or were they packages? By now so many doubts had been sown in my mind that I began to think that perhaps they were a bit bulky for just scribbled messages. And anyhow, why hadn't he just phoned? The police told me that I could now be prosecuted as an accomplice. The only thing that lightened the gloom was when they asked me whether Stephen had flashed money around. I had to laugh, Stephen was notorious for his meanness, but they couldn't, or wouldn't, believe that he had made his living from his patients and selling the occasional drawing, nor that his hand was the last out of the pocket when a round of drinks was called for.

And right in the middle of all that my luck really came to a standstill.

I was spending the evening with Paula at home with her younger brother John Hamilton-Marshall and a couple of West Indians. Paula and John were having a row over money – she supported him and didn't want to give him any more – but the row soon grew violent. I stuck up for Paula, and gave John a clout. He lost his temper and hit me back, hard enough to cut me across the eye. He stormed off and Olive, the housekeeper, managed to stop the bleeding. We thought we would all go out to The Allnighter.

I was first down the stairs and there, standing outside, was Lucky Gordon. He caught me by surprise and jumped on me, knocking me to the ground, punching my face and kicking me in the ribs. I was terrified after all his threats to get even with me for Johnny's slashing. Paula raced upstairs and dialled 999 while her two West Indian friends hauled Lucky off me. I ran screeching up the stairs with blood all over me – my eye had opened again and was even worse now. The two West Indians picked up my handbag and its scattered contents, slammed the door in Lucky's face and hot-footed it into the flat.

'It's okay,' said Paula, 'the police are on their way.'

'Christ!' said her friends. 'We can't get involved with the police, not now, what the hell are we going to do?' One of them was already on a possession charge, the other one muttered something about his wife being pregnant and any trouble with the police would upset her. They were black and knew what they were talking about; the law was never in their favour. We told them to hide in the bedroom and when the police arrived only Olive, Paula and myself were present. They took one look at the state I was in and called in a doctor; they were glad to have a chance to arrest Lucky at last though they didn't catch him till the following day. I thought I was going to breathe easy for a while but to our horror Stephen Ward bailed Lucky out. We were to find out why later.

From then on Lucky became the focal point of Burrows' and Herbert's questioning. How had I met him? Why had I gone there? And slowly the wheel turned back to Stephen, about how we had gone to the Rio cafe in Paddington for a lark, how I had met Lucky while looking for some pot. We talked about Stephen's interest in black girls. They probed deeper and deeper into Stephen and his sex life and with every answer the picture grew more sinister. The high heels that turned him on became a fetish, sending me down the road to the milk machine an attempt to put me on the streets. My mind became influenced by their interpretations and all our fun became filthy.

At the magistrate's hearing after Lucky's arrest I was asked if I knew two men called Comarchio and Fenton. I guessed these names referred to Paula's friends but I didn't know their surnames; they were Pete and Triller to me. They had rung a couple of times to make sure I was going to keep my promise, and so I told the court 'No, I didn't'.

Afterwards I was a bit worried. For one thing I hadn't known that Lucky knew the men, but he must have done for them to be mentioned at all. Lucky must have reasoned that if he called on them as witnesses they would have been forced to back his word, a fellow black man, against mine, a white girl. They could, in all fairness, say that I had already been injured earlier in the evening.

I took my worries to Burrows and Herbert. 'About those names mentioned . . . ' I ventured.

'Don't you worry about a thing, Christine. You did very well, everything went fine.' For once they weren't eager for my company. They looked at their watches and moved off before I could explain my doubts. Fool that I was, I took them at their word. By now I was a minor celebrity, appearing in the papers constantly and, as I photograph well, there was continued speculation on John Profumo's ability to resist my charms.

Around this time I met up with Robin, an old friend from my Dolphin Square days. He wanted to borrow some money to pay a drugs fine and I lent it to him from my *Daily Express* money. He knew a lot of people around town and suggested that I should capitalise on my fame. He would become my manager and we would start by writing my book together. I would talk into a tape-recorder and he would get the tapes transcribed. When the time came for the first session he dropped methedrine in my coffee. Did I talk! I couldn't stop – I didn't know anything about the drug but it wasn't nicknamed the truth drug for nothing. Robin found that he had stumbled on a very hot property indeed.

I enjoyed working with Robin a lot more than the prospect I had been offered of doing the same thing with Stephen. He had deteriorated very rapidly in the last few weeks. He didn't shave regularly any more, he no longer wore suits and never washed. He had never liked bathing ('it's bad for the skin, little baby,' he would explain to me) but he had always presented an immaculate appearance. He was also keeping very odd company; the painter Vasco Lazzolo had become his confidant now and none of his old friends dropped by Bryanston Square for coffee.

Ivanov had been whisked out of London in January, a few days after Stephen had told him of my contract with the *Sunday Pictorial*. I'm sure Stephen must have missed him as they had been very close. Eugene did not say goodbye and Stephen must have wondered just how one-sided the friendship had been. He had been used, the biter bit.

And so Glorious June arrived. What a misnomer for that summer of 1963.

Lucky Gordon's case started on the 5th at the Old Bailey with him pleading not guilty. Robin came with me. I was the chief witness with Paula and Olive as corroborators. To the question of whether there had been any other persons present I replied a dutiful 'No' to protect our frightened West Indian friends. It didn't seem a very important lie, and I was convinced there was plenty of evidence to convict Lucky and have him out of my way for years.

Halfway through the proceedings Lucky decided to dispense with his lawyer and conduct his defence himself. Immediately he started to rant and rave: I was a prostitute,

Stephen Ward was my ponce, I had given him VD, I had been pregnant by him. I was appalled and asked Robin to try and stop him. Robin sent a note to the judge but it made no difference. Lucky was allowed to continue his allegations that Stephen and I were depraved, that we performed our sex acts in front of each other and procured for each other. I didn't stop to think that some of the things he was saying were at least half-true. I stood up in court and shouted:

'Stop him, it's all lies, you can't let him go on, look, the press are taking it all down . . .'

'Send that woman out of court,' the judge ordered and I was bundled unceremoniously out while the press dutifully ran for the telephones.

Robin rang his solicitor, a Mr Lyons, who came round straight away to see what could be done. I sat in a little room, crying with shame and anger. Outside there were crowds waiting for a glimpse of me, not just the press but ordinary people just dying to point me out. Perhaps they thought it would be something to tell their grandchildren.

And right in the middle of it all came the news of John Profumo's resignation, admitting that we had had an affair and that he had lied to the House. It sounds cold and callous but, looking back, I can honestly say I felt nothing for him at that moment. To pretend compassion or sympathy now would be a downright lie.

All I could think of was the money I could now make. Robin was quick off the mark too and arranged for the *News of the World* to buy my story for £23,000, a whale of a sum in those days. We started work on it that very evening and I was far too busy being a star, in the centre of things, to give a thought to poor Jack's disgrace. I signed my contracts, including one with Robin, happily convinced that my future was secure and I could at last buy mum a house.

The following day Lucky was sentenced to three years'

imprisonment. Mr Lyons had taken me to court to hear the verdict and as Lucky was led away from the dock he hissed at me with hatred, 'I'll get you for this.' Mr Lyons insisted this be placed on record. I spent that evening with Robin and Alex Murray, who was going to write my book. There was something odd and secretive in the air; it was agreed that Alex should receive £15,000 for his work, but I was kept in the dark about why he should have such a large fee. I was suspicious and said I wouldn't sign anything more, I was going home. Robin tried to make me stay, saying Burrows had asked him to look after me. I phoned Burrows and he had said no such thing.

I demanded my tapes back from Robin and he said that if I was going to be that difficult he would burn them. He probably thought I wouldn't like to see all that hard work go up in flames but I made him do it. We burnt them in the bath.

I was still brooding about whether I was being double-crossed again the next evening when it was announced on the radio that Dr Stephen Ward had been arrested. It was a terrible shock, far more so than Profumo's resignation, though I should have known something was going to happen to him. On Burrows' and Herbert's last visit they had shown me a statement signed by Mandy that had mentioned an abortion. At that time even helping someone to obtain an abortion was a criminal offence, though Harley Street gynaecologists were making a fortune in discreet nursing homes. And Stephen and I had helped out a girl who had appealed to him, although it was only with telephone numbers and a bit of comfort. That wasn't good enough for the police, and they made my position very clear.

'Either you sign a similar statement or I think you might find yourself standing beside Stephen Ward in the dock,' was how they put it. I signed.

Stephen was charged with living off the immoral earnings

135

of myself, Mandy Rice-Davies and other women, of inciting me to procure girls under twenty-one for him to have unlawful sex with, of conspiring to effect an abortion and of keeping a brothel, all offences against the peace of our Sovereign Lady the Queen. Whoever had said 'Get him' must have had a very pleasant Saturday evening. I still had no idea that I was next on the list.

After the first shock I began to see how absurd the charges were. The picture of him haggling over prices for Mandy and I while his distinguished and titled friends sipped coffee in the sitting room would be laughed out of court. As for Mandy parting with a penny . . . she was tighter than Stephen. And even though they had statements that we had accepted money from some men, how could they turn buying the occasional tin of coffee or pound of sugar into something sinister?

The police opposed every application for bail right through the magistrates' hearings, which went on for almost a month. Life was absolute hell. I tried desperately to grasp what was going on. I soon realised I was the star witness but that this time there was no glamour attached to being a central figure. The questions I had answered at the police station were introduced as if they were brand new and all I was allowed to say was 'yes' or 'no'. I was never given a chance to explain or qualify, I wasn't permitted to speak to Stephen. I was kept apart from the other witnesses; I only knew Mandy in any case and even she couldn't hide her pleasure at being in the limelight.

The preliminary hearing was a public appetiser, and the papers devoted vast amounts of space to the case of the doctor and the vice-girls. Stephen was under a terrible strain and it showed through his eyes, though he maintained a cool demeanour sketching people in the court. I tried to comprehend what was going on but all I could understand was that the events that were happening to us were somehow planned. I could not in any way relate the charges against Stephen with Profumo or Ivanov. When I had finished giving my evidence I looked towards Stephen and he winked at me as if to say 'It's all right little baby', and I went outside and wept.

I tried to compose myself because I had another ordeal to face – the crowd outside. I had always held my head high, with never a hint of a tear or a trembling lip as I went from the building to the waiting car. This time there was the usual deathly hush as the door opened to let me out and I thought I could manage. Then a dog barked. The crowd took it as a cue. All of them leering, jeering and yapping at me. The humiliation was complete. They were letting me know that they thought I was a dirty little tart, no better than an old brass on the corner. I was branded.

The change in the climate of public opinion was not lost on Robin Drury. The ex-mistress of a member of the Cabinet was dramatic, salable stuff, a common prostitute was not going to be of much use to him. In any case Lucky's appeal had been granted, on the grounds that he would be able to produce the two witnesses he had been unable to find at the time of his trial. And the reason they were now prepared to come forward? You've guessed it. I now had money.

Robin was first in with a demand for £10,000. The tapes we had burned were not the real ones; he claimed he still had those. John Hamilton-Marshall had told his story to a paper for £500, saying it was he who had hit me and that Fenton and Comarchio were present. Comarchio was also being offered money from a paper to go to the police and tell them I had lied in court. They were all going to sell unless I paid.

I arranged to talk to Comarchio and Paula drove me to a meeting out of town. We sat in separate cars to discuss the matter. Comarchio needed the money for a barrister to get him off a petty charge. I pleaded that I had only lied for their sakes and that if Lucky went free my life would be in great danger. He pulled out a torn-off cigarette packet and a couple of names on it, not in his hand-writing. The names were Axon and Oxford: I had already heard of them, they were connected very heavily with the enquiries about Stephen and me. I told Comarchio that I hadn't received my money yet and that he wouldn't be seeing sixpence of it and the next day told Mr Lyons that we must see these policemen and confront them. Comarchio was trying to blackmail me but he was being manipulated by the police.

Mr Lyons also looked into the contract Robin had tried to make me sign the night we burned the fake tapes. It would have given him complete control over me – I could not have married without his permission, if he had booked me as a stripper in the Middle East, I would have had to have gone.

Everyone was scrabbling about for money, any story about me or Stephen could fetch a price. So much for friends. What we didn't need at that time was enemies, but we had them. Two bitter enemies in the forms of John Lewis and Michael Eddowes. Lewis' hatred was a personal one towards Stephen, which I hadn't helped; Eddowes' hatred was for the government. The scandal surrounding our names must be nurtured; the Profumo association, coupled with our newly revealed decadence, could only harm the Conservative Party. Any dirt clinging to either of us helped the Labour Party's chances at the next election, and backing Lucky's case was a sharp move on their part. Robin Drury passed on my tapes and they fell in George Wigg's lap. Years later someone said that Harold Wilson should have put my portrait in his home and given thanks each time he passed it. I was the magnificent pawn.

Stephen was allowed bail on 3 July at a recognizance of £3000. Paul Mann returned from Spain, playing the go-between again. The message from Stephen wasn't encouraging. It was basically that if I didn't stand up in court and blame the police for threatening me he would blow my case against Lucky, and I would be had up for wilfully organising his wrongful imprisonment. Something was going hideously wrong. I didn't believe Paul but drove to where Stephen was staying. When we got there I felt afraid to go in; I couldn't trust anyone any more. At that moment Stephen drove up, parked his car and walked towards mine.

'Come in and have a coffee, little baby,' he suggested. His face was unemotional but he looked so awful, nothing like the man who had been my laughing, light-hearted friend for whom I would have done anything, the brilliant osteopath who could cure a headache with a gentle massage of the neck, the quick-witted artist who delighted all he met. It had all gone, all the love, the caring, the excitement we had shared.

I shook my head. I couldn't face what was happening. I drove off and left him, and when I turned the corner the tears ran down my face. I stopped the car and sobbed over the wheel. It was the last time I spoke to him. I had deserted him, by then it was him or me.

If only we had known at that moment what we were up against. We should have stood together, clung together, held on to each other, but we didn't. We were both surrounded by liars, thieves, greed and spite and we were afraid, we couldn't even trust each other when we needed to. All we could do was behave like small cornered animals. It was tragic.

CHAPTER EIGHT

STEPHEN WARD's trial was set for 22 July, 1963, and the build up of the background was skilfully orchestrated.

On 21 June, while Stephen was still in custody, Lord Denning was invited by the Prime Minister to undertake an inquiry about whether Profumo's liaison with me could have endangered the nation's security. Around the same time a series of articles exposing the late Peter Rachman as the most evil, ruthless landlord ever to jangle a bunch of keys appeared, with lurid stories of rotting, rat-infested dwellings being let at exorbitant prices to the new immigrants from the West Indies. The stories never failed to draw attention to the fact that both Mandy and I had been his mistresses. So shocked and appalled by these reports was the Leader of the Opposition, Mr Wilson, that he tabled a debate in the Commons on the subject, right in the middle of Stephen's trial.

The cities of the world were agog with rumours of upper-crust orgies. Which Minister was the man with the mask became a favourite party guessing game; Duncan Sandys and Ernest Marples got the most votes. The 'in' people across two continents amused each other saying that in London 'It was food from Fortnum and Mason, drink from Justerini and Brooks, and girls from Stephen Ward.'

Stephen made one splendid last two-fingers gesture. He arranged for an exhibition of his work, including his portraits of the Royal Family and many famous faces, to open the same day as his trial – to pay the legal costs, he said. The royal pictures were deliberately highly priced, and a few days later Anthony Blunt walked into the gallery, handed over £5000, and walked out with all of them. Ironic in the light of recent events.

I didn't go to the exhibition. I wasn't enjoying the macabre carnival the way Mandy was, though, like her, on the first day of the trial I dressed myself to the nines for the occasion in a gold sleeveless dress with matching cape. Mr Lyons had hired a Rolls for me; after those earlier cat-calls I needed every bit of confidence I could muster. But a fat lot of good it did me. The judge, Sir Archie Marshall, a beady-eyed little man almost swamped by his ceremonial robes, glared at me balefully, and the opening speech of the prosecuting counsel, Mr Mervyn Griffith-Jones, drew such a vivid picture of Stephen's depravity, of foursomes, of two-way mirrors and houses of ill-repute, that one could be forgiven for thinking he was enjoying himself being able to say all these rude things out loud. The character formed by his speech was of a creep, a dirty old man who liked to defile young girls before passing them among his friends and collecting his share of their rewards.

I was put in the witness box and asked to swear the Truth, the whole Truth and nothing but . . . while some of the witnesses waiting outside had promised the police to do just the opposite. They asked me how I had met Stephen. Had he introduced me to Peter Rachman? We were off. Had Peter Rachman given me money?

'He kept me,' I replied firmly, which wasn't the answer they wanted at all. At that moment I felt like running away but couldn't. They were shocked that I had gone to bed with a man whose surname I couldn't remember. I could remember but didn't want to implicate Stephen, as it was a friend of his. Even Stephen's visits to Comeragh Road took on a sinister aspect under their scrutiny. If he had brought friends round, how many had I bedded and how much money had I received from them? They were going to have a field day with Mandy and Astor and the cheque for the rent. Poor old Major Eylan got dragged in to corroborate my denial that Stephen had introduced us. Very sweetly he tried to salvage my reputation by saying that although we had sex and he paid me, he also took me out to the theatre and restaurants and regarded me as a friend.

They went through my list of ex-lovers, always asking about money, until Mr James Burge, the defending counsel, intervened demanding to know where these questions were leading.

'We must establish whether this witness is a prostitute,' said the judge.

They had said it out loud, in front of the press and the overflowing public gallery. I was furious and called out: 'I would like to say that I am not a prostitute and never have been.'

'We'll come to that in due course,' he said stonily.

The prosecution were on to a new and condemning line. In quick succession they reeled off the names of Ivanov, Profumo, Eylan and Manu, prefacing each one with 'Did you have intercourse with?' To each I could only say 'yes'. The questions went straight on to whether anyone (not necessarily one of them) had ever helped me with my rent. Another 'yes' and I was cooked. And that mention of Ivanov and Profumo was the nearest we got to the origins of the police investigation. The threat of charging me with being a spy had been a sham to frighten me and I had fallen right in.

They then returned to how much money I had given Stephen. I told them I had lived rent free, was always borrowing from him, and usually only paid him half back. They couldn't understand a world where people took it in turns, where if you were flush you paid the bill, if you were

142

out with someone wealthy, they paid. They also couldn't see that organising a date for Stephen was not exactly a heinous crime, that the girl could always refuse his offer. He wasn't being accused of rape. They made him sound like a cross between Errol Flynn and Vladimir the Impaler (and there were plenty of women in the crowds outside panting for a try). Then it was Mr Burge's turn (if the two lawyers' roles had been swapped Stephen would have stood more of a chance) and he was altogether more civilised, establishing that it was more a case of living off Stephen than the other way round. He then suggested I could have made a lot of money as a prostitute if I had wanted to, a compliment I could well have done without right then.

Quite unexpectedly he changed the subject to Lucky Gordon's attack, asking whether I had said Comarchio and Fenton were not present. I agreed that was true, though I couldn't think what it had to do with Stephen's case. I didn't realise that I had been tricked into committing perjury again. Stephen had said he would get me through Lucky and I had walked into the trap. Lucky's appeal was to be heard on the thirtieth, and I did not know that my incriminating tapes had been passed on to the Attorney-General, Sir John Hobson.

The trial continued for eight days, creating sensational headlines for the newspapers. There were a couple of young girls whom I had introduced to Stephen but they both made it quite clear that they had enjoyed their brief affairs with him. Mandy was next in the witness box, very well schooled. She knew who she was going to mention and why. Douglas Fairbanks Jnr had his reputation ruined very neatly by her when her reply to why she had included him on her list was 'Because I don't like him'. She had already had the better of Lord Astor, who had denied their coupling before the court, with the now famous remark 'Well, he would, wouldn't he?' Dr Emil Savundra's name

143

was not mentioned; he was referred to as the 'Indian doctor' who paid Stephen's rent and Mandy's rates. Perhaps Fairbanks should have taken a leaf out of Savundra's cheque book. Money doesn't always talk.

If the public thought they had already caught more than a glimpse beyond the veil of respectability there were even greater surprises to come. Ronna Ricardo, a convicted prostitute, made an astounding statement from the witness box denying the truth of her evidence in the magistrates' court. She told the court she had been frightened by the police investigations, that they had kept her away from her baby for long hours and made it clear they had powers to have her young sister put in a remand home and her young brother put away for poncing. She had signed her statement just to go home to her family but the truth was that she had only gone round to Stephen's place once, and while she had had a few drinks and a foursome, it was not for money.

The sympathy for this courageous declaration in court was absolutely minimal. Inspector Herbert was called and asked if there had been any suggestion that a witness could find themselves in trouble if they didn't sign.

'I cannot recall so doing,' was the wooden reply. Poor Herbert, all that time spent getting me to recall past events must have affected his mind.

The interest in the next witness was absolutely maximal. She was everything a morally upright public expected a tart to be. Slaggy and sleazy, according to the police she had been 'found' soliciting on 4 July (the day after Stephen was allowed bail) and while going through her handbag they had discovered Ward's name amongst half a dozen others in her diary. She, Vickie Barrett, then claimed that she had known Ward for two and a half months, ever since he picked her up in Oxford Street. He had driven her back to Bryanston Mews where there was a man waiting in the bedroom. Stephen told her to get on with it and that he had

144

collected the money already. Afterwards Ward had proposed that she returned in a few days' time to oblige some of his friends who had more unusual tastes – they preferred a good beating with whips or canes to sexual intercourse. These saucy little spanking parties were held once or twice a week for the benefit of middle-aged and elderly men friends of Stephen's. It conjured up a gleeful picture of a bedful of shiny, bouncing British buttocks in the eyes of a delighted world. It also conjured up a keen question from Mr Griffith-Jones.

'For the whipping, what is the market price?'

'£1 a stroke,' said Vickie, and I thought of all the barristers who had partaken in the orgies Stephen used to attend and wondered if this was a little discreet market research. Vickie Barrett then went on to say that Stephen had kept her money in a little drawer for safety. She also said that she had known nothing about Stephen's case when she was stopped by the police and nobody queried this. As though a girl on the game wouldn't be round there looking for her money double fast! There was a lot of scepticism in court about this wondrously convenient find by the police, except from the righteous side of the bench of course.

Stephen admitted in his evidence that he had picked her up, had sketched her and screwed her, and paid for it. But it was in reference to her story, while being cross-examined, that he began to crack. He shouted that anybody could be brought in off the street to tell lies about him, and it was true. The police had questioned 144 people about Stephen's sex life and they could have easily coaxed anyone into relaying a likely story.

The oddest thing about Vickie Barrett's tale was that while it swung public opinion towards an awareness that this was a blatantly put-up job, only I knew there was an element of truth in it. Stephen had always been excited by other people's need to substitute pain for sex (which is funny when you think they came to him to be healed) but I had also spoken to an unknown girl on the phone some time in the spring. It was already well known round our little community that Stephen was getting wilder all the time, that instead of wanting pretty young girls to escort and play with he preferred some really debauched numbers that he never took anywhere. But the girl who had answered the phone that day had confided in me and told me that Stephen was keeping her money for her. Did I think that was all right? Even then I thought it was Stephen up to his mean old tricks, anxious to hang on to his money and pay her back when he had a lump sum. Vickie also mentioned Vasco Lazzolo in her evidence and he had become Stephen's partner in adventures since the departure of Ivanov and myself.

It has been said that the incidents couldn't have taken place because of the police surveillance but that would have been just the stimulation Stephen enjoyed – getting away with it on one hand and creating a new set of cronies on the other. And a new set he certainly needed. Not one of the people who had spent happy afternoons in Wimpole Mews gossiping and talking on every subject, or those who had driven to Cliveden for a sunny day in the garden, had come forward as a character witness. Bill Astor had even reclaimed the cottage. The judge was careful to point to this cruel ostracism by his friends in high places as he began his summing up on Tuesday, 30 July. Stephen's public humiliation was complete. He could have taken being accused of being a spy, which would have acknowledged his access to men of power, but he could not take being labelled a ponce.

During the afternoon the news came through that Lucky Gordon's appeal had been upheld. I knew then that I was next. When the judge rose, adjourning the remainder of his summing up till the following day, I looked at Stephen. We were both defeated; our adventure, which had started so stylishly with the trip to Cliveden, had come to a sordid end. Lucky Gordon, slashings, shootings, drugs, Stephen Ward and Christine Keeler were now words inextricably mingled in people's minds. We were both feared and despised.

Stephen was staying in Chelsea with a friend, Noel Howard-Jones, during the trial. That evening he sat down and wrote a batch of letters, explaining to Noel that they were to be delivered if the case went against him tomorrow. They had dinner, then he drove a girlfriend, Julie Gulliver, to her home saying 'goodbye' rather than his usual 'see you', one of those small phrases to haunt a person forever. He drove around alone till he guessed Noel had gone to bed, then he quietly swallowed a bottle of Nembutal. When Noel found him in the morning he was hardly breathing at all. His letter to Noel was typically charming and apologetic; he must have smiled to himself as he mentioned the fact that the car needed oil in the gear-box. It was such a casual way to go.

I heard when I got to court for the summing up. So did the judge. He immediately revoked the bail but by then Stephen was well on his way out of Sir Archie Marshall's reach. He was in a coma for three days, but this did not deter the law of the land from passing judgement. The judge continued his good work by pointing out that 'abnormal sexual activity' (i.e. Vickie Barrett's flagellation job) was not, according to current law, prostitution. Only the exchange of bodies for normal intercourse with payment in return constituted that. Quite simply he was telling them that since Mandy and I had received money for a screw and had paid our way at Stephen's house with our earnings, he was a ponce and we were two prostitutes.

147

And the jury found him guilty of living off our immoral earnings in part, but not off any of the girls who had been convicted for soliciting.

Stephen died on 3 August, leaving his 'little baby' branded for life. But at that moment I couldn't give a twopenny cuss for what the world thought of me. I had lost the best friend I had ever had, or would ever have. For the three days he lay between life and death I cried, prayed and begged for his life to be restored. The night he died my phone rang. 'How's your conscience now?' said a cultured voice.

So they blamed me, a silly girl whose life Stephen had moulded, because I had been forced to bear witness against him. They, in their London clubs, were blameless.

My mind was a monstrous madness of the mistakes we had made, the missed opportunities, the manoeuvres that had not been ours. Everything I have said about Stephen Ward in this book is true; he was a complex, amoral, intelligent, indulgent man and worth a million of those stuffed-shirt bastards who were grateful for his outrageous wit and mental freedom when it helped them unleash their inhibitions, but slunk away when he needed their help. To them Stephen was always a bit of an outsider; he was too inquisitive, he knew too much and yet not quite enough, and they closed ranks when Stephen got too close for comfort.

And the sad thing is that so did we, his other set of friends, his young girlfriends. Only it was we who knew too much and yet not enough. Nobody knew how to handle Stephen. Today he would be totally acceptable as wickedly camp; he was a man before his time. He strove to manipulate the Foreign Office, the Law, and people's sex lives, but in the end he was defeated by all of them.

I remember going to buy a paper when he was dying. Just as I got to the news-stand someone, a stranger, glanced at the headlines and said: 'Oh, Ward, the ponce?' I felt such a hatred I tried to drive Kim and myself into a wall, taking two entirely innocent people crossing the road with us. It was a hatred that was to take me five years to rid myself of.

Maintaining my hatred wasn't difficult. I had a lot of help, mostly from the police, ex-lovers and lawyers. It started even before Stephen was dead. The film producers and Mr Lyons were insisting that I flew to Germany to start the film that Stephen had written, *The Christine Keeler Story*. They kept ringing me to tell me he was recovering though the bulletins were saying the opposite. It was immaterial to them whether he lived or died, my film test had been successful and I was under contract. It is extraordinary to look back on the ruthlessness of those times. I was, after all, a 21-year-old girl who had just gone through an amazing six months of court appearances, slashings, shootings, fame, shame, and now Stephen's death, and I wasn't expected to have any feelings at all. My body rescued me with a totally exhausting attack of asthma, something to which I am still prone. They made the film anyhow, with Yvonne Buchanan playing my part.

I didn't have too much time to worry about it as I was about to embark on another role myself. I was having a bath when there was a heavy bang on the door. Even the innocent recognise the sound of the Law and I had been warned to expect them. It is that moment when you mentally call them the law, not the police, that you know you are going to be standing in the dock quite soon.

'Who is it?' I called, wrapping myself in a towel and knowing damn well.

'Detective Axon,' came the reply. He'd come for his pound of flesh. There were three of them, Detectives Axon and Oxford and a policewoman who followed me into the bedroom while I got dressed. At that moment the zipper on my dress stuck and the scene turned to farce with each of them taking it in turns to tug, push and ease the zipper up my back. Nobody knew whether to giggle or to swear but eventually they got me through the door where the press were waiting for the next Keeler saga.

I had thought I was quite familiar with Marylebone Police Station but being banged up in a cell was a new one on me. Mr Lyons, who had warned me this was likely to happen, had told me to say nothing unless he was present. They tried to question me but I kept silent, insisting that they call him. My relationship with the workings of law and order had undergone a severe change during the last few months.

Mr Lyons tried to get me out on bail that night but they refused. I was soon joined by Paula and Olive, who were very frightened but told me that Fenton, Comarchio's partner was also incarcerated in one of the cells. That got me worried. I had been keeping Fenton quiet by giving him one, something the police might well translate into 'interfering' with a witness. I had to get him out quickly before he talked. Normally my voice is deep and low but it wasn't that night. I ranted and hollered until they let me speak to Mr Lyons, and though they listened carefully while I explained he must make sure to get all of us out on bail in the morning they fortunately didn't get the gist.

At the preliminary hearing the line-up against me was overwhelming and sickening. There was Lucky who had loved me, Robin Drury who had shopped me out of revenge, Comarchio who denied attempted blackmail and John Hamilton-Marshall who had hit me and was willing to stand up and say so even though it would send his own sister to jail. What an engaging gaggle of men I had met in the last two years! Paula, Olive and I were sent for trial on conspiracy to obstruct the course of justice, for causing Lucky Gordon to be wrongfully arrested, maliciously accusing Comarchio of blackmail and perjury. The date was set for 6 December, 1963. I was advised that if I pleaded guilty on the conspiracy and perjury charges I would get six months and the other charges would be dropped. I was also told that if I didn't take the proffered advice the weight of public opinion was running so high against me I would be likely to receive two years.

I set out to enjoy my last few weeks of freedom by going to discos like the Ad Lib, a nightclub above the Prince Charles Theatre, where the walls were lined with mock mink and a tank full of piranha fish entertained the tanked-up guests. It was owned by young Lord Tim Willoughby and the customers were bright and talented actors, pop stars and models. The Swinging Sixties had begun.

There was one more odd event before my trial. Mr Lyons called me one day to say that he had heard there was a man going round Fleet Street claiming to be my real father and trying to flog his story. The man had contacted him and wanted to meet me. It was a real jolt. My father belonged to my very first memory, that of being taken into a hospital to visit a man lying in bed with a bandage round his tummy; he had had his appendix removed and for some reason that was all I remembered of him. I must have seen him at other times (though my mother had left him when I was young) but this picture stuck.

I wasn't too sure about seeing him again. It felt disloyal to my mum and my stepfather who had been marvellous to me all through this horrible year but I was curious. I was suspicious too. Why this sudden interest in a daughter he had never tried to contact? Could it be that I now had money? Curiosity won and I invited him to my new house in Linhope Street, Mr Lyons insisting on being there just in case. He walked through the door with his arms wide open but I wasn't anyone's little girl any more. I shook hands. He had brought his girlfriend with him and she was about my age, which didn't help the long-lost father image much.

But he was uncannily like me. We even sat and moved in the same way. I knew very little about him. I half understood that my mother had left him because he was wild and unreliable, but she had never wanted to speak of him so I was uncomfortably fascinated to listen to him tell me about himself.

He was adopted and brought up by the Keelers but he had tracked his mother down. She had written to him (he had the letter with him) and told him that his father was a full-blooded Red Indian and that she was a young Irish girl working on the reservation.

'You've got my blood in you,' he told me, 'a wild streak, and you will never settle down, you'll be like me.' I shuddered at the time and didn't want to hear any more, and instead of feeling proud of my heritage I felt ashamed. So ashamed that this is the first time I have ever owned up, not even all the times people have commented on my high cheekbones that must come directly from my grandfather. The thought of having the blood of two fighting nations running through my veins was not encouraging and the streak of wildness was all too familiar. I wanted to settle down; I was even contemplating marrying a young business-man called Mark and my father's words boded ill to that ambition. I didn't ask him about trying to sell his story but when he came to my trial with two reporters I wouldn't see him. But I felt happy that I had given my parents enough money to buy a shop in Somerset and stay away. I wouldn't have upset them for the world.

On 6 December I received the full benefit of British justice. I had not been attacked by Lucky Gordon and I had lied to the courts to protect people whom I hardly knew at the time from police action. I was sentenced to nine months' imprisonment, Paula to six months. Fenton was bound over for three years and Comarchio was already inside for his drugs offence. And Lucky was free. Yet I actually felt a sense of relief at the prospect of being shut away from the public gaze. It was a signal that the dreadful year was over, the violence, the hassles, the hatreds, the fears and the tragedies were all going to be left behind. I would be safe in prison, it would give me time to sort out the terribly confused state I was in. I wouldn't have to wear make-up and be *that* Christine Keeler, I could throw my false eyelashes away and try to find *me*.

Paula wept but I could find no tears, I had shed too many over Stephen. I turned to my lawyer and said:

'Don't you realise that in a few months it will all be over, my life will be my own again?'

'I wouldn't be too sure, Christine,' he said cautiously. 'You may never be able to throw off the effects of the last two years.'

'Nonsense,' I replied confidently as I was led away. I was going to be free of blackmailers, sharks and Lucky's threats. I would have a house and money to come out to, one of the points of pleading guilty being that none of the bastards could come at me for money. My parents were safe, though they had had to change their name. I signed a form that gave Mr Lyons power of attorney over my properties, film and book rights, and entered Holloway fully aware that the world thought I had got my just deserts at last.

I suppose in those last few weeks I must have been thinking of prison in terms of a sort of super rest-home, an asylum. Certainly nothing had prepared me for the reality of the madhouse I entered that day. My fame had gone before me and as I was led through the wing where the prostitutes and alcoholics were kept I was greeted by a cacophony of tin trays banging against bars and the foulest, filthiest language I had ever heard. Nicely brought-up girls did not swear like fishwives till much later in the Sixties, unless that's what they were, gutter people, so it came as a shock. I didn't feel half as brave as I had in court but I was determined not to cry or bow my head.

I spent the first night in the prison hospital and the next day was allocated a cell and kitted out with a prison uniform: grey woollen skirt, grey blouse, grey jumper and grey bloomers to match. A long way from my Maurice Krevatz tailor-mades but I was allowed to keep my 'waspie' (a suspender belt that clinched the waist) and by the time I had tapered the skirt I felt quite neat and presentable. I was put in the wing for first offenders and a prison officer was delegated to keep an eye on me for the first few days. They were called screws, which wasn't the way I used the word, and I had heard enough about lesbianism in women's prisons to make sure there wasn't going to be any mix-up in its usage.

She never left me alone, taking me for the customary finger-printing, blood tests, VD and crabs inspection, bustling me to the head of the queue and causing great resentment. Then I was informed that I had to take an IQ test and that was the limit. I could accept, with a certain passive dignity, that they were temporarily in charge of my body but they weren't going to have my mind as well.

I sat before the psychiatrist maintaining a stolid silence while she tried to coax me into co-operation. Suddenly she snapped.

'You think you're very smart, don't you? You think you have a big name and you're a cut above everyone else. Well I don't think you're smart at all, look at you, all you've done is get yourself in prison.'

That did it. I burst into tears. I, who had been determined never to cry again, ran screaming and sobbing from the room, banging my head against the walls, saying over and over again, 'What has happened to my life, what have I done, I don't understand.'

The psychiatrist fetched me back and said she was sorry,

but she had to say those things to make me break, that to bottle pent-up emotions in prison was dangerous and could lead to a complete nervous breakdown later.

I passed my test with flying colours and was given a job in the library, but I soon asked for a transfer to another job because here I was stared at and whispered about just as much as outside. I really did want to be alone. They gave me a job scrubbing the floors of my wing which I didn't mind, even though they thought they had got me on my knees at last. But they hadn't. I squatted on the job instead.

Prison wasn't, on the whole, too bad, a bit like a girls' boarding school really. But, as in most institutions, there is always one who has it in for you. Unlike most first offenders I was not transferred to an open prison, partly on my mother's advice. 'She'll only run away,' she had told the Governor, and she was right. My stepfather was physically ill with the worry of this last year, so much so that he had taken to his bed and lost two stone. I would have been off like a shot to see him. So I was to pass my full sentence in Holloway and made to work stitching shirts. It was boring, the highlight of the day being the five minutes' chat you were allowed when the scissors had been put away before you were returned to your cell. The screw who hated me ordered me to sit down during this sacred break and I told her the scissors had been collected and turned my back on her. I was put on report and marched off to the 'dungeon', a bare room with a mattress on the floor, nothing else. There you wait till the Governor deigns to see you. Then you get the full judicial performance, the governor behind a vast desk, surrounded by screws while she listens to the reporting officer exaggerate your minor misdemeanour into practically causing a riot. I was fined a shilling a week for three weeks and decided that with my temper it would be safer for me not to be in a room with that fat, peroxided old bag so I went back to scrubbing floors. It was peaceful and gave me access to the kitchen where I was asked to look after four budgies.

One was completely bald on his chest but by the end of five months of my loving care he was quite splendidly feathered again. I loved those budgies and if I had stayed in any longer I would have been in danger of turning into the Birdgirl of Holloway. As it was, when I left I asked if I could take them with me, and guess what? They belonged to my enemy screw.

The other thing that kept me going were the letters and visits from my parents. My stepfather had been forced from his bed by a good old-fashioned country doctor who had taken one look at him and said, 'Get up. You are not helping anyone like this.' So he did as he was told and started getting better at once. Their letters were funny and bright, telling me which plants would be in bloom for my return, the awful escapades my daft dog, Bruce, got into. All the time I could feel their pain trying not to burst through yet they never once chided or blamed me. Their love sustained me.

I needed this sustenance. There was a spate of threatening anonymous letters sent to both Holloway and to my defending counsel, Jeremy Hutchinson, which made me recognise the truth of Mr Lyons' comment that perhaps I could never escape the consequences of the last two years. I began to be afraid and hid myself in books, reading all the works of Emil Zola and John Steinbeck.

I had one good laugh through one of Mr Lyons' visits. Apparently a mutual friend had bumped into Michael Lambton at a party and, far from his association with me upsetting his business, his reputation had been enhanced by having been engaged to Miss Keeler. He had to give up drink in order to deal with the challenge. What a laugh, but at least it was one way of repaying my 'loans'.

My hopes that the drudgery of prison would dampen my

156

ardour for adventure in the future were wiped out by an incident when I had been there about four months. I had taken to working in the garden in my spare time just to keep busy. I was supervised by a 'red band', one of the women prisoners the screws think they can trust, and one day she surreptitiously handed me a note. For a moment I thought it was going to be a love note from her . . . but, no, it was from a male prisoner from another prison who had the job of painting our roof. The note said he thought I was the greatest in the world and after months without any male attention I flipped. I was in love again. I started to brush my hair with special care and come alive again.

I sent my Prince Charming a little note via my trusted red band. The next morning I was on report again, back in the dungeon and then up before the Governor, my note spread before her. It was hardly deathless prose. It said 'Hi, I think you're great. Are you married? If not give me your telephone number so I can ring you when I get out. Love C.'

You would have thought they might at least have taken note of my improvement in prison; at least I had asked if he was married. But no, I lost three days' remission. So, in a place almost as safe as a nunnery I could still get into trouble over a man.

CHAPTER NINE

THAT DAY in June 1964, when I stepped outside the gates of Holloway, I was shaking with fear. Any hopes that I had had, that the world outside would have found someone else to focus on, were already dashed. I had to be smuggled out the back way to avoid the crowd of press photographers and, possibly, the authors of the threatening letters. In prison I had felt safe but now I had to face public opinion again and I felt the destruction for which I had so long been blamed pressing in on me. Mr Lyons whisked me off to a cottage he had rented by the seaside where my parents were waiting for me, but I knew I was soon going to have to start living again. But how to begin? I had no training, no skills except perhaps in the art of pleasing men, and I had given myself a solemn promise that I would never do that again. And there was no longer Stephen to run home to in times of trouble.

First of all I had to learn to live alone. Luckily I didn't have any money worries at the time, but I was terrified of going out. The shame of prison and being classed as a prostitute went very deep. I felt like a wounded animal and slunk away to hide. I even wore a wig to go to the cinema; the film was *Tom Jones* but I couldn't enjoy it, so sure was I that the audience would spot me and start pointing and hissing. I couldn't appreciate that they were too enthralled to worry about me, I was too paranoid, I had no self-confidence at all.

I think I stayed in a sort of state of shock for about five years. It certainly took that long for me to assess what I had done. I remember a reporter asking me for my views on Election Day when the Conservatives lost, and my reply dumbfounded him.

'Why ask me, it's nothing to do with me,' I replied airily, and I meant it. The events of the previous year had not sunk in and for a long time I thought people were being silly when they suggested that I had been a key figure in toppling the government. It was also a long time before I could comprehend that the famous Profumo/Keeler Affair was a watershed in people's attitudes; the mid-Sixties with its sexual freedom, pop music and fashions all released a whole generation of young people who happily turned their backs on stuffed shirts and fuddy-duddies.

I got myself a boyfriend, and this time the word 'boy' was truly applicable. He was sixteen and was his mum mad! Freddie was related to Charlie, the brother of Ronnie and Reggie Kray and they were very kind to me, persuading me to go out with them. They took me to the Society Club (now Tramp) and, of course, nobody would have dared say a word against me in their presence. Freddie lived with me for over a year and we had a lot of fun, he was very protective even though I once broke his heart. He came home unexpectedly and found me in bed with Ringo Starr. Poor lad, he was so overwhelmed at meeting his idol that he couldn't say a thing. It was a pretty fiery relationship; I was always chucking him out, then inviting him back again.

One day when I had thrown him out I discovered him at the Ad Lib with a woman who was a madame and she sent me a little note saying, 'Don't be jealous Christine, I can get you five hundred pounds a time'. I was so furious I drove straight down to my parents who now had a bungalow at Wokingham, crashed my car and stayed there. I met up with a girlfriend and told her that I wanted to get married.

Could she introduce me to some marriageable men? The first man she set me up with seemed ideal; he was charming, had money and brought me flowers. For a whole week I had him lined up. Then we went to bed together. I was back hammering on Jackie's door the next day, demanding that she find me a bigger one. She did, and seven weeks later I married Jim Levermore who was a labourer. A week later I discovered I was pregnant.

We were happy for a while, a very little while, but I still couldn't get away from being Christine Keeler. There were rows with the Press Council over my wedding day pictures and once again I emerged as a money-grabbing, limelight-seeking young woman, though it was Mr Lyons who had organised the payments. The press also printed my address which I had begged them not to and, sure enough, on Valentine's Day I received a card from Lucky. That was it for me. Jim and I weren't getting on, he didn't trust me because I *was* Christine Keeler and his unfounded jealousy led him to play silly, macho games with other women. We broke up before young Jimmy was born and though we had another stab at marriage it was all over within a year.

My mother was recovering from cancer of the womb and the doctors said they would not know for a year whether it would return. The one thing that kept her mind off her worries was looking after Jimmy, so it was agreed that I would come back to London and she would bring him up. As I spent every weekend there it wasn't too much of a wrench.

I found a flat in Weymouth Street and soon after that, a new man – a New Zealander called Michael Nelson, who also very soon started giving me the run around. It was the same mixture of pride and distrust that men seem to suffer from as soon as they hitch up with me. I am a symbol to them, not of femaleness but of their male achievement. They can boast that I am their girlfriend, knowing that it makes them attractive to other women on the assumption that anybody who can satisfy me, the Great Strumpet, must be good in bed. Michael flaunted his unfaithfulness, not caring how much he hurt me. I had still not recovered my self-confidence and finally screwed two of his best friends out of revenge. He was shattered when he found out; he had obviously not heard about the sauce for the goose being equally good for the gander and promptly took his bruised ego back to New Zealand.

About that time I discovered The Star, a pub in Belgravia run by a marvellous man, Paddy Kennedy. He was famous for his foul language and it was in his bar that I found the safety from the public attention I had been seeking. Everyone who drank there was somewhat larger than life and he was the greatest of them all. If anyone had dared to stare at me and point me out he would have felled them with his rich and fruity use of Anglo-Saxon. It was the first time in over two years that I was able to go to a place on my own. He made me feel like a person again.

I moved into a flat in the mews where the pub was situated and felt strong enough to go through all the newspaper clippings my mother had kept. I wanted to write a book in order to study just exactly what had happened to me in 1963, and began finally to understand things that had been obvious to others. I was also meeting a lot of marvellous people at Paddy's: Robert Mitchum, who had been my idol for years, came to my parties as did Clint Eastwood. Peter Sellers was anxious to add me to his list of achievements but I didn't want to know, neither did I with Roman Polanski, but I was grateful for their regard. They gave me a sense of belonging, that there was a place where my streak of wildness was welcome. My London was a whirl: Alvaro's, the Aretusa, the Revolution, hell-raising actors like Peter O'Toole, Mike Pratt and anybody who happened to be around. We all danced a lot; I loved to show

161

off by now, and we drank and laughed a lot. People were always changing partners and it didn't seem to matter, I had a brief fling with Dudley Moore but I wasn't dependent on any one man. David Bailey took my picture, which was very flattering because he was very choosy, and I was asked everywhere. I met Steve Abrahams who was the head of the Flower People and went to work for Release on a voluntary basis. Release had been founded by Caroline Coon and was a centre for young people with drugs problems. I was just a backroom girl and I kept reports on what happened to the young people after their treatment or a brush with the police. Some of the kids' stories were heart-breaking: there was an eighteen-year-old who hanged himself in his cell while awaiting trial. It all seemed so wrong as a lot of the people I knew smoked dope, including me, but it was the kids who got caught and sentenced to prison. My experience there was still vivid and my heart was filled with pity.

And all the time I had plenty of beaux and a lot more offers. I met up again with some of my Arab friends and went to dinner at the Dorchester with King Hussein and felt very grand. The oddest thing of all was my friendship with Sarah Macmillan who lived nearby and also frequented The Star. It was from her that I learned that her father, Harold Macmillan, had once said, 'The worst mistake I ever made in my political career was calling her a tart.' It was then that she explained that anything to do with sex was abhorrent to her father though she never did know if he or Lord Boothby was really her parent.

It is ironic that Macmillan should have blamed himself for calling me a tart because I had been just that, though I couldn't own up even to myself at the time. I was writing my book, studying the Denning Report and other books written at the time, but I couldn't bring myself to admit the real truth, that however much I had listened to Stephen assuring me that prostitution was a mental attitude, giving sex for money was just that. I missed Stephen and still do, I missed his humour and fun, but I began to see he had been an unfortunate influence on my life. People often say I am a destructive influence on the lives of the men I love, but if this is so I think some of the blame must go back to Stephen, whose guidance was not exactly healthy for a young girl. To this day I cannot really think of him as a bad man but I wish I had never been mixed up in his sexual and political manoeuvres. My own life might have stood a better chance. As it was, there were a couple of rich young men who wanted to marry me, one was titled and the other heir to an enormous fortune, but as soon as their families heard of their intentions they were very firmly whisked away as if there had never been scandals in such great families.

When the second one had been recalled to the bosom of the family I was mortified, especially as they had deliberately asked a former girl of his to stay with them. So I went out to find myself a substitute. It wasn't difficult; my reputation and my looks combined to make a fatal fascination and Antony Platt was a handsome man. Having suitably stung my erstwhile fiancé's pride I wickedly invited Antony to a dinner party at a friend's, using our lack of a record player as an excuse. The dinner was atrocious but Antony was marvellous and from then on he courted me, taking me to the opera and dinner at the Savoy. Seven weeks later I married him and was instantly pregnant again. Antony was rich, with a large house in Chelsea, and the kind of man Stephen would have approved of.

I should have been happy at last, but I still had to face being Christine Keeler and sort out my life. I left Antony seventeen times during our short marriage.

Fortunately I had kept my flat so I had a bolt-hole. I found marriage claustrophobic, and there is something about the sight of a man's clothes in my wardrobe that

163

drives me mad, I don't know why. I nearly died giving birth to Seymour, whom I named after Mr Lyons who had looked after me all through the years, setting up companies and managing my constant change of homes. Antony was very proud of his son and organised nannies and home helps so that I would have nothing to do. I couldn't stand it; my life wasn't my own, and even my son was hardly my own, so efficient was the help. Six months later I left everything, the house, my credit cards, my car, and took my son to live with me alone. I wanted to look after him myself. The fight over custody of Seymour was filthy as was our divorce, but for once I had something to fight for and I won.

But it was against a background of ultimate disillusion; I discovered that I didn't have a penny. The first I knew of it was an income tax demand for £33,000; nothing had been paid for eight years. I had given Mr Lyons complete power of attorney before I went to prison and he had handled all my finances since then, collecting royalties from newspaper features, photographs and the publication of quick-turnovr books which bore my name and sold in Japan and France. I had always signed the documents that he asked me to, but mysteriously all the money had been banked abroad. There was a hell of a legal wrangle with the revenue people on my side but I still ended up penniless. I hated Mr Lyons more than anyone in the world; I had trusted him as if he were my father, he had rescued me from Robin Drury's clutches, he had known intimately the ordeal I had suffered, but then quite deliberately he had let me down. He had taken 78% of all my money so cleverly that I had no chance of getting it back.

On top of that Antony went bankrupt so I couldn't even get decent alimony. Seymour has spent his childhood in poverty, just like his mother. After one of the custody hearings which had dragged in my associations with black people in the past, a lawyer said to me 'Christine, that is what all the cases against you have been about. Prejudice.' It's true, there are still plenty of people around who have only to see me talking to a black man to think 'She's at it again'. In fact I have only had one affair with a black man since my second divorce; he was a barrister (which makes it all right in some people's minds) but I still have many black friends. I saw Lucky once about five years ago; Frank, who owned the Rio, arranged a meeting and it passed off uneventfully. I suppose we were both older and had learned something.

Of the other people in my saga, I have never seen John Profumo since though I did receive a message from him indirectly. I was having a drink in an afternoon club in Soho when a young man who played the piano there approached me and told me that he was Jack's godson. I wondered for a minute if he wanted to follow in his godfather's footsteps but no, he had a message that Jack would like to see me again sometime. I don't know when Jack had made this rather indiscreet overture but the timing of its delivery was somewhat unfortunate, as the Lord Lambton scandal had just broken.

'No thanks,' I said firmly. 'He caused me enough trouble last time.'

Laying blame is always a wasteful process but looking back I do think that John Profumo should have known better. He was a grown man with a responsible job, he knew of Stephen's reputation as a gossip yet he still asked him for my number, and he had seen me go off with Eugene Ivanov, with whom for all he knew I could have been having a torrid love affair. I know there is an old saying that a standing cock has no conscience but he should have stayed away from temptation. I know he has paid his dues to society since but poor Stephen never got the chance to pay his. Ruining my life may not seem very important to some, considering what I was, just a pretty scrubber, but I have paid dearly for that overwhelming desire of his. I am forever *that* Christine Keeler.

Mandy has fared better financially than I, but she was always shrewd with money. I sometimes wonder if she really believes she went to grand dinners at Cliveden and met Nancy Astor. I know damn well she didn't even go to the pool, let alone the house, and as for meeting Paul Getty . . . well, they say you need imagination to be an actress.

We have only met once over the years, when she came to stay for a couple of days with her daughter on one of her trips to Israel. You can't not like Mandy, everyone does, but there is too much in our shared background that she wants to hide for us ever to be close friends again. Not just our naughty exploits but our reponsibility towards Stephen's disgrace and death. .

Most of the others are dead too: Bill Astor, Mr Lyons (who died soon after I screamed that I would get him for what he had done to me), many of the people who were Stephen's visitors. Of the girls in Stephen's case I know nothing, but Paula and Kim are still good friends – in fact my girlfriends have been far more constant than the men in my life. There have been plenty of those, I am happy to say, and those I have not mentioned can please themselves whether they feel grateful or insulted at being left out. Just blame my bad memory.

There is a bitter irony in the fact that the girl who started out in life using men and screwing them should end up alone and penniless, the men having used and screwed her. Perhaps Stephen was right when he said, 'Don't take the easy way out, little baby', though that is exactly what he did do. He didn't have a lot of choice; he would have got three to five years and he was too old to take it and there would have been nothing to come out to. I like to think that Stephen's death was in some way responsible for the less

166

judgemental attitudes towards sex and society that grew up in the Sixties. Certainly his case alerted the public to the knowledge that they were supporting a Them and Us society and they changed it. I wonder what he would think of the widespread pornography that is so freely available now, of the orgies plainly advertised in 'contact' magazines? He would probably laugh, dismiss them and be bored; it was the secrecy that was fun.

It is not easy living your life being other people's clichés; most people only vaguely remember the facts and it has become fashionable to regard me as a victim. Well, yes, I was a victim of the circumstances that shot my name into the headlines and a victim of a section of society's revenge for upsetting their applecart, but equally I was a victim of my looks, my sexuality and my own complete inability to discern the difference between the shits and the good men. All my sufferings have come through men.

I now realise I would rather be alone than live with a man I have to pretend with. I have married friends who spend their lives playing games of jealousy, fighting all the time to keep their passion alive. I do not want to go through such charades just for the sake of a screw in order to hang on to my womanly feelings. Nor do I want to be with a man who understands my womanly feelings but whom I don't want to make love to. There are plenty of them about.

Both my marriages failed through my husbands' feeble-spiritedness. They could not accept that I loved them and had to prove that they were as desirable as my reputation led them to believe I was. One of them was rich and the other poor but it made no difference, they each wanted to punish me for what had gone before. They wanted to hurt me and they did, so I ran away.

I would dearly love to meet a man I liked and could learn to love utterly, someone who would help me protect my hard-won self respect, someone who recognises that women have changed over the last twenty years. I do not want to be pliable any more, just for the sake of a regular screw and a roof over my head. When I made myself promise I would have no more sex for money, I meant it inside marriage as well as out. I've kept my promise, though my financial circumstances have made it very tempting sometimes. I could have reasoned that since I was branded anyhow I might as well get the benefit, but I didn't. That doesn't make a saint out of me, I've still had the odd, wicked fling, even a couple of threesomes when things got particularly wild, but it's always been for my own pleasure, not for money. I cannot be bought again. That was part of growing up, and mine was a lesson never to forget. It is sad that the male ego is such a fragile thing, that men feel the constant need to prove themselves regardless of who they hurt in the process. It's true that I have thoroughly enjoyed helping a lot of them boost that same ego. I find now I want to get to know a man before I trust him with my body and my feelings. I do not want one who will use my love against me, not ever again, but I think that such persons are very rare.

I would like my sons to grow into such men. With Jimmy, my eldest, I shall have to work hard to gain his confidence when he feels ready to turn to me but Seymour, who is now ten years old, already has trust in me – one that is mutual. I think it is best to be honest with one's children; after all, they don't miss a thing, so both my sons know who their mother is. When they are old enough they can make up their own minds about my life story. They will probably have to make a few mistakes themselves before they can fully understand.

If Seymour doesn't like what I am doing, and doesn't trust the company I am keeping, he feels sure enough of me to say so and I listen to him. We talk about it and if he is adamant I take his advice. After all, nobody cares about you more than your children.

I would like them both to become helpful members of society, doctors, lawyers (honest ones) or actors perhaps, people who give something to life. I don't want them to be cheats, entrepreneurs who exploit other people, nor so morally upright that they despise and disregard others.

But that is all in the future and they are bound to rebel at some times, to get into scrapes even if they haven't inherited the wild streak from their mother. But I hope they won't pay the same price that I did.

NEL BESTSELLERS

T51277	'THE NUMBER OF THE BEAST'	*Robert Heinlein*	£2.25
T50777	STRANGER IN A STRANGE LAND	*Robert Heinlein*	£1.75
T51382	FAIR WARNING	*Simpson & Burger*	£1.75
T52478	CAPTAIN BLOOD	*Michael Blodgett*	£1.75
T50246	THE TOP OF THE HILL	*Irwin Shaw*	£1.95
T49620	RICH MAN, POOR MAN	*Irwin Shaw*	£1.60
T51609	MAYDAY	*Thomas H. Block*	£1.75
T54071	MATCHING PAIR	*George G. Gilman*	£1.50
T45773	CLAIRE RAYNER'S LIFEGUIDE		£2.50
T53709	PUBLIC MURDERS	*Bill Granger*	£1.75
T53679	THE PREGNANT WOMAN'S		
	BEAUTY BOOK	*Gloria Natale*	£1.25
T49817	MEMORIES OF ANOTHER DAY	*Harold Robbins*	£1.95
T50807	79 PARK AVENUE	*Harold Robbins*	£1.75
T50149	THE INHERITORS	*Harold Robbins*	£1.75
T53231	THE DARK	*James Herbert*	£1.50
T43245	THE FOG	*James Herbert*	£1.50
T53296	THE RATS	*James Herbert*	£1.50
T45528	THE STAND	*Stephen King*	£1.75
T50874	CARRIE	*Stephen King*	£1.50
T51722	DUNE	*Frank Herbert*	£1.75
T51552	DEVIL'S GUARD	*Robert Elford*	£1.50
T52575	THE MIXED BLESSING	*Helen Van Slyke*	£1.75
T38602	THE APOCALYPSE	*Jeffrey Konvitz*	95p

NEL P.O. BOX 11, FALMOUTH TR10 9EN, CORNWALL

Postage Charge:

U.K. Customers 45p for the first book plus 20p for the second book and 14p for each additional book ordered to a maximum charge of £1.63.

B.F.P.O. & EIRE Customers 45p for the first book plus 20p for the second book and 14p for the next 7 books; thereafter 8p per book.

Overseas Customers 75p for the first book and 21p per copy for each additional book.

Please send cheque or postal order (no currency).

Name ....

Address ....

....

Title ....

While every effort is made to keep prices steady, it is sometimes necessary to increase prices at short notice. New English Library reserve the right to show on covers and charge new retail prices which may differ from those advertised in the text or elsewhere.(7)